The Iraq War

Other Books in the Social Issues Firsthand Series:

SOCIAL ISSUES
FIRSTHAND

The Iraq War

Ronald D. Lankford, Jr., Book Editor

GREENHAVEN PRESS
A part of Gale, Cengage Learning

GALE
CENGAGE Learning™

Detroit • New York • San Francisco • New Haven, Conn • Waterville, Maine • London

Christine Nasso, *Publisher*
Elizabeth Des Chenes, *Managing Editor*

© 2010 Greenhaven Press, a part of Gale, Cengage Learning.

Gale and Greenhaven Press are registered trademarks used herein under license.

For more information, contact:
Greenhaven Press
27500 Drake Rd.
Farmington Hills, MI 48331-3535
Or you can visit our Internet site at gale.cengage.com

For product information and technology assistance, contact us at

Gale Customer Support, 1-800-877-4253
For permission to use material from this text or product, submit all requests online at
www.cengage.com/permissions

Further permissions questions can be emailed to permissionrequest@cengage.com

Articles in Greenhaven Press anthologies are often edited for length to meet page require-ments. In addition, original titles of these works are changed to clearly present the main thesis and to explicitly indicate the author's opinion. Every effort is made to ensure that Greenhaven Press accurately reflects the original intent of the authors. Every effort has been made to trace the owners of copyrighted material.

Cover image © Pavel Bernshtam, 2010. Used under license from Shutterstock.com.

LIBRARY OF CONGRESS CATALOGING-IN-PUBLICATION DATA

The Iraq War / Ronald D. Lankford, Jr., book editor.
    p. cm. -- (Social issues firsthand)
  Includes bibliographical references and index.
  ISBN 978-0-7377-5010-2 (hardcover)
  1. Iraq War, 2003---Juvenile literature. I. Lankford, Ronald D., 1962-
  DS79.763.I763 2010
  956.7044'3--dc22
                                                2010007133

Printed in the United States of America
1 2 3 4 5 6 7 14 13 12 11 10

Contents

Chapter 1: The Iraq War Zone

Chapter 2: The American Home Front

Chapter 3: The Debate on the Iraq War

Foreword

Social issues are often viewed in abstract terms. Pressing challenges such as poverty, homelessness, and addiction are viewed as problems to be defined and solved. Politicians, social scientists, and other experts engage in debates about the extent of the problems, their causes, and how best to remedy them. Often overlooked in these discussions is the human dimension of the issue. Behind every policy debate over poverty, homelessness, and substance abuse, for example, are real people struggling to make ends meet, to survive life on the streets, and to overcome addiction to drugs and alcohol. Their stories are ubiquitous and compelling. They are the stories of everyday people—perhaps your own family members or friends—and yet they rarely influence the debates taking place in state capitols, the national Congress, or the courts.

The disparity between the public debate and private experience of social issues is well illustrated by looking at the topic of poverty. Each year the U.S. Census Bureau establishes a poverty threshold. A household with an income below the threshold is defined as poor, while a household with an income above the threshold is considered able to live on a basic subsistence level. For example, in 2003 a family of two was considered poor if its income was less than $12,015; a family of four was defined as poor if its income was less than $18,810. Based on this system, the bureau estimates that 35.9 million Americans (12.5 percent of the population) lived below the poverty line in 2003, including 12.9 million children below the age of eighteen.

Commentators disagree about what these statistics mean. Social activists insist that the huge number of officially poor Americans translates into human suffering. Even many families that have incomes above the threshold, they maintain, are likely to be struggling to get by. Other commentators insist that the statistics exaggerate the problem of poverty in the United States. Compared to people in developing countries, they point out, most so-called poor families have a high quality of life. As stated by journalist Fidelis Iyebote, "Cars are owned by 70 percent of 'poor' households. . . . Color televisions belong to 97 percent of the 'poor' [and] videocassette recorders belong to nearly 75 percent. . . . Sixty-four percent have microwave ovens, half own a stereo system, and over a quarter possess an automatic dishwasher."

However, this debate over the poverty threshold and what it means is likely irrelevant to a person living in poverty. Simply put, poor people do not need the government to tell them whether they are poor. They can see it in the stack of bills they cannot pay. They are aware of it when they are forced to choose between paying rent or buying food for their children. They become painfully conscious of it when they lose their homes and are forced to live in their cars or on the streets. Indeed, the written stories of poor people define the meaning of poverty more vividly than a government bureaucracy could ever hope to. Narratives composed by the poor describe losing jobs due to injury or mental illness, depict horrific tales of childhood abuse and spousal violence, recount the loss of friends and family members. They evoke the slipping away of social supports and government assistance, the descent into substance abuse and addiction, the harsh realities of life on the streets. These are the perspectives on poverty that are too often omitted from discussions over the extent of the problem and how to solve it.

Greenhaven Press's *Social Issues Firsthand* series provides a forum for the often-overlooked human perspectives on society's most divisive topics of debate. Each volume focuses on one social issue and presents a collection of ten to sixteen narratives by those who have had personal involvement with the topic. Extra care has been taken to include a diverse range of perspectives. For example, in the volume on adoption, readers will find the stories of birth parents who have made an adoption plan, adoptive parents, and adoptees themselves. After exposure to these varied points of view, the reader will have a clearer understanding that adoption is an intense, emotional experience full of joyous highs and painful lows for all concerned.

The debate surrounding embryonic stem cell research illustrates the moral and ethical pressure that the public brings to bear on the scientific community. However, while nonexperts often criticize scientists for not considering the potential negative impact of their work, ironically the public's reaction against such discoveries can produce harmful results as well. For example, although the outcry against embryonic stem cell research in the United States has resulted in fewer embryos being destroyed, those with Parkinson's, such as actor Michael J. Fox, have argued that prohibiting the development of new stem cell lines ultimately will prevent a timely cure for the disease that is killing Fox and thousands of others.

Each book in the series contains several features that enhance its usefulness, including an in-depth introduction, an annotated table of contents, bibliographies for further research, a list of organizations to contact, and a thorough index. These elements—combined with the poignant voices of people touched by tragedy and triumph—make the *Social Issues Firsthand* series a valuable resource for research on today's topics of political discussion.

Introduction

The Iraq War, or the Second Gulf War, began on March 20, 2003, when a military force, primarily consisting of soldiers from the United States and the United Kingdom (U.K.), invaded Iraq. The United States president, George W. Bush, initiated the assault in an attempt to remove the Iraqi leader, Saddam Hussein, from power and to recover any weapons of mass destruction. Many public officials also viewed the Iraq War as a response to the September 11, 2001, terrorist attacks on the United States. As of March 2010, the United States continues to occupy Iraq and battle insurgents.

One aspect of the Iraq War that has become less noticed as the war has continued is the human dimension as experienced by the soldiers and civilians on both sides of the conflict. While it remains common for news agencies to report on the number of deaths of soldiers, the reported number of civilian deaths in Iraq has been less reliable. There has also been controversy over how the U.S. military calculates many statistics, such as the reporting, or lack thereof, of noncombat-related injuries. When one looks at the number of combat and civilian deaths, the number of noncombat injuries, and the ongoing impact of physical and psychological injuries resulting from the conflict, the broad human dimension of the Iraq War becomes more evident.

The coalition force that initially invaded Iraq in 2003 consisted of approximately 297,000 personnel. Initially, the United States deployed 67,700 soldiers in Iraq in 2003, a number that climbed to 157,800 in 2008. The United Kingdom initially deployed 47,000 soldiers, and a smaller number of troops were deployed by more than twenty nations, including Honduras (368), New Zealand (61), and the Dominican Republic (302). Over time, Iraqi Security Forces would replace much of the international force, and countries such as the United Kingdom would withdraw troops.

As of November 2009, there had been 4,684 U.S. soldiers killed in Iraq, according to CNN; for United Kingdom troops, there had been 179 deaths during the same time period. There had also been approximately 139 deaths of soldiers from other countries, including Bulgaria, the Czech Republic, El Salvador, Estonia, Fiji, Georgia, Hungary, Italy, Kazakhstan, Latvia, the Netherlands, Poland, Romania, Slovakia, South Korea, Spain, Thailand, and Ukraine. These numbers include both combat and noncombat deaths. Since the beginning of the Iraq War, approximately 100 to 175 American soldiers have died of noncombat-related causes each year, including accidents, suicide, illness, and, in rare cases, murder.

For every Coalition soldier killed in Iraq, many more have been wounded or injured or have contracted illnesses. As of October 2009, the Iraq Coalition Casualty Count reported that 31,557 U.S. soldiers had been wounded in Iraq since the beginning of the war in 2003. The U.K. statistics are divided into several categories and include 3,598 field hospital admissions and 1,971 aeromed evacuations (air ambulance evacuation), according to the British Ministry of Defense.

One controversy concerning U.S. troops has focused on the accusation that many injuries remain unreported. In 2004, for instance, United Press International's investigations editor, Mark Benjamin, noted that there were 17,000 injured or ill U.S. soldiers who had to be evacuated out of Afghanistan and Iraq, but that none of these cases appeared on the Pentagon's casualty list. More recently, the Department of Defense has reported that as many as 360,000 veterans of Iraq and Afghanistan may have suffered serious brain injuries, when these injuries had previously been listed as mild concussions. Other soldiers have contracted illnesses, such as the Gulf War syndrome, while still others have been exposed to toxic chemicals, such as sodium dichromate.

While it was clear that there would be civilian casualties in the Iraq War, it has been difficult to validate the number of these casualties. Likewise, it has sometimes been difficult to separate civilian casualties caused by Coalition forces and those instigated by insurgents in Iraq. Primarily, civilian death counts have been based on media reports, hospital activity, and found bodies.

The organization Iraq Body Count, which has documented civilian deaths in Iraq since 2003, reports that its "public database includes deaths caused by U.S.-led Coalition forces and paramilitary or criminal attacks by others."[1] As of November 2009, Iraq Body Count estimated the number of civilian deaths in Iraq relating to the current war to fall somewhere between 94,231 and 102,820. A survey by the medical journal *The Lancet* in 2006, however, estimated as many as 654,965 Iraqi deaths resulting from the war. Many non-Iraqi civilians working in Iraq have also lost their lives. An early November 2009 report by Iraq Body Count, for instance, listed 6 deaths, including an oil company employee. The Committee to Protect Journalists has also reported that 141 reporters have been killed during the Gulf Wars since 1992.

The human dimension of the Iraq War continues to unfold. At the beginning of 2009, U.S. president Barack Obama announced that U.S. troops would be gradually reduced in Iraq, leaving a force of approximately 4,100 soldiers by 2011. While many of these troops would be allowed to return to the United States, many would possibly be deployed to Afghanistan, where the president planned to increase troop levels.

Many soldiers and civilians will continue to struggle with the aftereffects of the Iraq War. The viewpoints in *Social Issues Firsthand: The Iraq War* offer a variety of firsthand perspectives on this unfortunate conflict.

Note

1. "About Iraq Body Count," Iraq Body Count, November 2009 (retrieved). http://www.iraqbodycount.org/about/.

SOCIAL ISSUES
FIRSTHAND

CHAPTER 1

The Iraq War Zone

Civilians Prepare for War

Thura al-Windawi

The following selection has been taken from the journal of Thura al-Windawi, a nineteen-year-old Iraqi who chronicled her and her family's experiences as the Iraq War began in March 2003. Living in Baghdad, al-Windawi reports her family's preparations before the American and British airstrikes on March 20, and their attempt to remain safe. Just before the bombing, she notes, Baghdad looked like a ghost town. After gathering together with her uncles and grandmother, al-Windawi reports hearing shots in the street and bombs falling at night: the Iraq War had begun.

W*ednesday, 19 March 2003*

Dear Diary,

Today was a long day. My mother woke me and said this was the day we had to go to Granny's house until my sisters get used to all the noise of the missiles and explosions and gunfire, and the boom of the planes flying overhead. It'll be scary for the little ones at first, so they've got to be able to get used to it gradually or they'll suffer the effects for a long time afterwards.

We went to the pharmacy today to buy my diabetic sister, Aula, some insulin, but the shelves were empty, and the pharmacist said that insulin is in short supply. We ended up buying six months' worth from four or five different chemists. We also managed to find her blood-test kits and some new needles—a special kind that don't hurt so much when she injects herself. It was very expensive, but we don't care about the money we have to spend to get what my sister needs, because money comes and goes, but who will replace my sister if I lose her? Aula can't eat sweets or chocolate, which she loves so much, because of her illness, and in Iraq you can't buy sweets or sugar-free treats for diabetics. We keep Aula's insulin in a fridge belonging to a friend of Dad's who's got his own private generator.

Leaving Home

As a family we want to be together, but we decided Dad will stay here to watch the house and we—my mother, two sisters and me—will go to Granny's. Aula has been crying. She doesn't want Dad to stay at home alone: she wants him to come with us. But we can't leave the house empty for long periods of time—we might get burgled, or with all the bombing there could be a problem with the water and electricity. This house is all we've got and it wouldn't be easy to replace.

The most secure room in the house is Dad's study, so we helped to prepare the house for him before we left. We pushed his heavy desk in front of the main door so robbers could not come in. Our two dogs, Bambash and Max, went to our neighbour's house.

We packed food, trainers [sneakers], medicine, face masks (in case of a chemical-weapon attack by either side in the war) and potassium citrate, which you take if you get poisoned by gas.

Dad's promised to come and visit us from time to time. How long are we going to be at Granny's house? I think the best thing is for us to spend tonight there, at least; that way there'll be lots of us all together, so we won't be frightened by the sound of the first missiles falling. Granny will be there and so will four of my uncles with their wives and my cousins. We'll all keep each other's spirits up and we'll feel safer with my uncles around. It'll be easy to keep my little sister,

Sama, occupied, too. She'll be able to play with the other children, unaware of the danger all around us.

The Quiet Before the Storm

These are the last hours before the bombing, and everything is changing fast. My friends are all staying home. Some are talking about weapons of mass destruction, and electronic bombs which ruin electricity and water supplies and give people terrible headaches.

I am so worried about these last bombs. Maybe girls who aren't married yet will have trouble getting pregnant because of them. Maybe pregnant women will suffer. I have heard that after these bombs fall, people seem drunk even though they have not been drinking. What will happen to these people?

All the shops and streets are empty. The windows are bricked up. The new ice-cream shop, Penguin, already has broken windows. The government ministries are empty. We are waiting.

I am suddenly seeing things as I never saw them before. This is the hardest day of my life. What am I going to see? People are saying goodbye to each other . . . We are like the *Titanic* going down, drowning in the ocean.

I felt sad as I closed my bedroom door tonight, thinking how much I'm going to miss being able to spend time there and sleep in my own warm, cosy bed. I feel like a writer without pen or paper to express what's going on inside her . . . I hope I get to come back soon.

(Later) The beautiful streets of the capital don't look normal any more. In most squares and at most road junctions, soldiers have taken up positions surrounded by sandbags. On the way to Granny's house I could see people going off to say goodbye to their friends and relations. Others were still stocking up for the war; they looked like little ants laying aside a store of food for the winter. It reminded me of when I last went to the market. The place was packed, and everyone was buying all sorts of things in huge quantities. The stallholders had so many customers they had to serve each one as quickly as they could. People particularly wanted tins of tomato paste—it's a basic ingredient of most Iraqi dishes. Imported goods like dried food, canned things, toothpaste, soap, cotton, tissues and bottled water have started disappearing from the shops. I just hope God will save us and keep us together. I will try to write every day so the world will know what happened here.

First Day of Shock and Awe

Thursday, 20 March 2003

Dear Diary,

It's 9:02 p.m. There is shooting outside from the Iraqi army. [Iraqi dictator] Saddam Hussein is on TV talking about the missiles dropped on Mosul by British planes. Missiles are also falling in Kuwait. Things are not normal here. The whole family is crowded together in my uncle Ahmed's bedroom at Granny's house, watching TV. We've called my uncle Mouhamad in Malaysia and he gave us some news. He says the Americans ran away from Umm Qasr, a port city in Iraq. Granny said it's bedtime, so me and my mum and sisters have gone into Granny's room.

(Later) Uncle Ahmed, who'd been out, came back to Granny's and told us that there is a government building burning in the street near Arasat, one of Baghdad's smartest districts. I hear and feel the first missiles exploding—when the earth shakes, your whole body shakes as well. What's going to happen to us? There is only fear in my house. Aula hid herself in Mum's arms because she feared the war. Her face looked scared, her eyes were wide and her body was shaking. Mum tried to calm her down. Sama slept through the whole thing.

A little while later everything went quiet outside, and all of us in Granny's room were silent, too. Granny told everyone to go back to bed. We were all looking at each other calmly but no one said anything, although there were all sorts of questions going through our minds. Everyone looked confused. 'I don't want any of you to be afraid,' Granny said. 'We're going to be hearing noises like these all day, every day, so we'd better get used to them.' We all respect Granny and love her so much. She's a very strong woman. When my grandfather died, she brought up my five uncles and my mother on her own, and she has seen many wars. She kept telling us not to be afraid and to control our tempers, as 'there is so much more to come'.

Uncle Ahmed served as a conscript [drafted soldier] for years, in the war with Iran during the 1980s. 'Don't be scared,' he said to us, 'it's nothing to worry about. Just a few fireworks going off, that's all.' He knows a lot about missiles, having been a soldier, and he was only trying to cheer us up. But I know perfectly well that the missiles aren't fireworks: they've been sent to kill and destroy, not for fun.

B-52 Bombers

(Later) The B-52s came tonight, but they've now accomplished their horrible mission and it's time for bed. I've still got the sound of their engines ringing in my ears. The explosions made an incredible racket, and each time they sent out great gusts of wind that blew the curtains about. Even though it's cold outside, we've left all the windows open because we're afraid the force of the blasts might smash them and send the glass flying into our faces.

I'm in a bed made up on the floor, covered with a thick blanket. I don't know if I'm shaking because of the cold or the fear. I can still feel the pressure of the bombs in my ears. All the children are asleep in the same room. My aunt is watching them so if they wake up they will not be afraid. My uncles are sleeping together and Granny is ordering everyone around.

Poor Mum is very worried about Dad. I understand how she is feeling but she won't say anything. She doesn't want anyone else to experience what she is going through.

The bombs are starting again. They're falling harder. We just wrap ourselves up in blankets to keep warm, and hope for the best.

Invading Iraq

Mike Ryan

In the following selection, Mike Ryan has reprinted the recollections of a British Royal Air Force (RAF) pilot—wing commander Moose Poole—who took part in the invasion of Baghdad on March 21, 2003. Poole narrates his 2,000-mile round-trip to Baghdad, one that includes refueling in the middle of the ocean, bad weather, and minimal radio contact. Through numerous difficulties, however, Poole reaches Baghdad and releases his precision bombs before returning his jet to the base.

COMBAT REPORT

Night One—21 March 2003 by RAF Tornado Pilot, Wing Commander 'Moose' Poole MA.

It was a straight forward night *sortie* [flight mission] as op [operations] missions go. Find a tanker, get some fuel, press to the target, drop some bombs, find another tanker to get enough fuel to land back at the base we started from. The KISS principle (Keep It Simple, Stupid) is always a good one to follow, yet there are times when even that isn't going to be enough—times when a huge slice of luck is definitely needed.

'The pre take-off preparations went reasonably smoothly, though I made life uncomfortable for myself by whacking my head on one of the undercarriage doors whilst doing the weapons checks. Fortunately, there was no blood, but the pain was an unnecessary "extra" on such a long mission. As soon as we taxied, it became clear that getting off the ground was going to take a bit more planning. With aircraft everywhere, both four-ships [groups of four fighter jets that fly together] were

Mike Ryan, *Baghdad or Bust: The Inside Story of Gulf War 2.* S. Yorkshire, United Kingdom: Leo Cooper, an imprint of Pen & Sword Books Ltd., 2003. Copyright © Mike Ryan 2003. Reproduced by permission.

baulked [blocked in] by US fighters doing their final arming checks. I sat in the lead of the second four, my access to the runway blocked by four F-15Es, the back pair of my formation behind two "blacks", as the F-117s are called. With gridlock similar to a Monday morning in Central London, I enquired over the radio whether the Eagles would like to get a "wiggle on" (a move on), as time was pressing. Finally they got out of the way and we launched on a round trip of 2,000 nautical miles, twelve minutes late.'

Flying up the Gulf

'On the equivalent of the Hammersmith flyover, we joined the "commuters" flying up the Gulf, all in search of the mission critical tankers. Fortunately, the pre-arranged traffic flow meant that although we couldn't raise anybody on the radios apart from the Navy, this didn't matter—at this stage, anyway. For the ensuing tanker "goat" (a word used for getting fuel from a tanker), radios were to play their part.

'We arrived at the refuelling rendezvous (RV) some four minutes late, short of fuel and with no idea where the tankers were. With zero help from AWACS [Airborne Warning and Control System planes] due to poor radio performance, no air-to-air TACAN (Tactical Aid to Navigation) and several options to choose from on the radar, it seemed highly likely that we would be spending the night on a remote strip in Saudi Arabia, having failed to complete the mission.

'My number two aircraft, with Dozy and Humpo on board, with a note of increasing concern, declared that they were really down on fuel. So are we, fellas—where the f--- are the tankers?

'Dozy spotted them on his night vision goggles (NVG) and called out: "Left 9 o'clock". The blob I was chasing on the radar was clearly not one of ours. We snapped left, giving our wingman some interesting challenges to remain in close formation—every man for himself in a situation like this. What a wonderful sight it is, when you've run out of fuel and ideas, to see those fuel hoses in your 12 o'clock [above]—I'd rather be lucky than good. Still unable to talk to the tanker on the radio, we joined and plugged in, finally speaking to him on a totally different frequency. Only then did we find out that he was well down on the plan and that he couldn't give us as much as we needed. I heard the back pair join on the second tanker—God knows how they had stayed in, with us manoeuvring so much. Bouncing around on the top of the weather made refuelling particularly difficult and having taken several attempts ourselves, I watched young Dozy joust on the left hose. The weather was awful. Extreme turbulence made the trailing hose leap all over the place, as though possessed by demons. After some ten minutes, he got in, by which time we had taken our now limited fuel and were ready to go. Number Four had suffered a computer failure and, though refuelled, was not in a fit state to push. We decided to press on with just Number Three, being unable to wait for Dozy who had valiantly managed to get his fuel in the most extreme tanking conditions I have ever witnessed.'

Bombing Baghdad

'So Moose (yes, another one!) and I and Lager and Jock pressed on. Still five minutes late, we had no catch-up on the four ahead. The radio situation didn't improve—we were still unable to raise the AWACS with the limited range of our Havequick radio, and where we were going it was unlikely to get better.

'As we pressed north, with radars on and with warning receivers showing little activity, we watched the bombing of Baghdad. Explosions under the cloud cover looked like the sort of light show Jean Michel Jarre [a French musician known for spectacular effects at outdoor concerts] might use, only this outdoor concert wasn't at Houston. Imagining the soundtrack, we watched missiles streak into the air in a volley of desperation, blindly hoping to find a coalition aircraft.

'After what seemed like eons, we reached the target. Always a tense place to be—the simplest of tasks becomes difficult as you struggle to funnel and restrain the adrenaline and get on with the job in hand. The training in the RAF is second to none—and boy do you depend on what has become your instinct when the enemy are shooting at you! There is no time to think what needs to be done, you need to do it automatically. We proceeded to pepper the target with precision strikes against carefully calculated pressure points—I was not surprised to see the Iraqis respond, albeit in vain. The missiles were never going to reach us, but at the time it takes some self-convincing, as you watch the mesmerising glow of each rocket motor eventually fade. Willing the jet higher and faster, we took what seemed an eternity to egress [get out]. We were vulnerable up here—should they be bold enough to launch fighters against us and whilst we had cover around, it would take a few minutes to get to us. Thankfully, that threat did not materialise and we slogged our way home, hoping the aircraft's engines would continue to put up with the strain. That the Tornado does so well at medium level is a blessing as it was designed for high speed, automatic terrain following at very low level; its natural environment. Apart from more firework displays and another light show, the push south to the tanker towlines was reasonably quiet. Still nobody to talk to on the radios, so a good chance of a repeat of the first tanker goat—the Saudi night stop beckoned once more. We could hear the formation ahead, and having noted the frequency earlier, made remarkably easy radio contact with our flying petrol stations. The weather had clearly not improved and despite having them on the radar and the TACAN, we did not see the tankers until we were within a mile of them. Another jousting session was made easier when they were persuaded to climb above the weather. There was no shortage of giveaway fuel this time and we took enough to get home, with a healthy reserve.'

Returning to Base

'The recovery was uneventful, even to the point where I was finally able to talk to someone on the Havequick and pass them our in-flight report: as tasked, successful (apart from 2 and 4). Disappointing for those guys to have had bad luck on the way in but then, sh-- happens.

'On landing, we discovered more than five hours after our departure, that Number Four had diverted with additional fuel problems—it really wasn't their night, so it was just as well they didn't push. As we got together with the front four-ship and debriefed the engineers, the banter and chat was wild and colourful. Only two of us had flown in the first [Persian Gulf] war and we smiled at the fevered exchanges of the other dozen aircrew. It hadn't been as bad as night one of Desert Storm by a long way, but the risks and the dangers are still very real.'

Keeping the Peace

Jonathan Moss

Jonathan Moss, a U.S. Army officer from Paris, Texas, relates in the following selection the dangers of leading a security force in Iraq following the bombing of a mosque (a Muslim house of worship) in the city of Samarra by Sunni (a Muslim sect) extremists in 2006. Remembering the aftermath of the bombing, Moss narrates his attempts to protect his unit from mob violence and to prevent an escalation of the violence. Moss also expresses his desire to return home and his fear that the next generation of Americans will also have to fight in Iraq.

The destruction of Samarra's Al Askari mosque [by Sunni extremists] on February 22 [2006] set off a wave of unrest across the country, and news of sectarian clashes has been pouring incessantly out of Iraq ever since. The Najaf province remains relatively calm, but that's not to say that tensions haven't increased. Anger toward Americans is more palpable; on convoys, people might spit or throw rocks at you, and this is a new development here.

When I first heard about the Samarra bombing, I was having a meeting with the mayor of Manathera, just south of Najaf. The Al Askari mosque is one of the holiest sites for Shiites [a sect of Islam]; I knew immediately that people were going to be enraged. Although Samarra is a distance north from Manathera, my immediate concern was my team. It's difficult to communicate our vulnerabilities in this situation, but try to imagine riding with your friends through downtown Austin [Texas] surrounded by a thousand or more angry maniacs throwing rocks and firebombs at you. Once a single vehicle is disabled, you're pretty much toast. I was trained as a lieuten-

Jonathan Moss, "There's More Violence Every Day," *Texas Monthly*, vol. 34, May, 2006, pp. 38–39. Copyright 2006 Texas Monthly, Inc. Reproduced by permission.

ant to always visualize the worst possible thing that can happen and then take all measures to prevent it.

Our three-Humvee convoy was outside the mayor's office pulling [working as] security while I conducted the meeting. His office is in a cul-de-sac, meaning there's only one way out. The exit leads straight into the heart of town; behind the office in the other direction is the Euphrates River. I asked the mayor, "Do you think we should leave?" "No, no" he answered. "You are safe here. No one harm you. Let's go look at the schools." He was guiding me back toward my original purpose for being there, which was to get recommendations from him about potential renovation projects for the city. I felt a little reassured, but in the back of my mind, all I kept thinking about was how the bombing was a really big deal. As far as I could recall, nothing like this had happened before.

A Brewing Storm

We took a stroll in the neighborhood next to the mayor's compound, and as we walked, I heard the loudspeaker click on at the nearby mosque. Anyone who has spent time in the Middle East is familiar with the call to prayer, and I always find myself wishing I knew what the callers were saying. This time there was no doubt. "Allah akhbar! Allah akhbar! Allah akhbar!" an unmistakable phrase that means "God is great," over and over again. Finally, the caller moved on to something else, and I asked my interpreter what he was saying. It was a call for gathering and demonstration, and my interpreter told me, "Don't worry, Captain. It's for peaceful demonstration only." That was good to hear. We checked out a couple projects, and then it was time to return to the forward operating base.

On our way home, we took the main road, which heads north through Najaf. I had assumed there'd be no problem with this, because any demonstrations would occur to the west, near the city's main shrine. Well, I was wrong. As our convoy drove right into the heart of town, we passed the mosque of [radical cleric] Muqtada al-Sadr and his Mahdi militia. Muqtada's claim to authority is his lineage. His father was Muhammad Sadiq al-Sadr, who was allegedly assassinated at Saddam Hussein's orders for political defiance. Muqtada has leveraged his family's courage for his own gain, and although he suffered militarily at the hands of the U.S. in 2004, the people in Najaf still hold him up as a leader. It's always easy to recognize his guys—they're the ones dressed in black. On that day, they were gathered en masse between his mosque and the road. Traffic was very thick, and we were quickly wrapped into the middle of it, sitting still directly in front of the mosque.

"Americans Get Out!"

As I looked to my left, I saw all the demonstrators watching us, waving their arms and chanting in unison. My interpreter, who is a Shia Muslim from Najaf, said with a smile, "Oh, sh-- Captain. They're saying, 'Americans, get out! Americans, get out!'" To be honest with you, that was exactly what I'd had in mind too. As I flipped the switch on my Humvee's siren, a call came up on the radio from one of our soldiers. "Hey, they're throwing rocks at us. What do we do?" Instantly I had an image of one of the young, inexperienced soldiers popping off a round unnecessarily and us being directly involved in a nightmare of potentially international proportions. Fortunately, one of the NCOs [noncommissioned officers] quickly answered up with the solution: "Nothing. We're getting out of here." Soon we were happily out of town.

A few days later, during a visit to Hurriya, a town a few miles east of Najaf, a demonstration of teenage boys broke out while we toured two schools. My interpreter told me that their signs condemned the bombing and implied that our nation was involved in the act. After our tour ended, I told the mayor, "Please tell your people that we had nothing to do with that attack. Tell them that our nation has offered to rebuild the mosque and that we want stability and peace in Iraq." He said, "Please, don't tell me these things like I don't know. Anybody who has a mind understands these things. Unfortunately, in this place there are things over which I have no control." What he was telling me should have already been obvious, but what I was seeing firsthand were the signs of a larger power struggle. The battlefield in Iraq goes beyond the city streets; it is being waged in the minds of these people. It's a terribly serious game, being played by people who have demonstrated a willingness to ignore the rules of their own religion. It's unlikely that we can win by trying to be equally ruthless, and when we give in to temptation and abandon the moral high ground, then we end up hurting the people we say we want to help. So what we are left with is an intractable riddle.

Having been here for several months now, I can say that I've honed my wish list down to a few things. One, I wish I could go home. Two, I wish I could get some good Mexican food. And three, I wish the Iraqis would sort this mess out. My fear is that our children will have to be involved in this fight when they come of age, and my sense is that if we abandon this place now, the fight in the future will only be more savage. I hope that I am wrong.

Visiting a Friend in War-Torn Iraq

Hannah Allam

In the following selection, journalist Hannah Allam visits an old friend who is now a medic in the U.S. military serving in Iraq. As Allam reunites with her friend, she realizes how difficult it is for Americans to be separated from family back home and wonders whether the war has changed her friend. At the end of her journal entry, Allam shares several of the letters that her friend has sent to her husband and daughter in the United States. In these letters, the friend relates her interaction with Iraqis and other American soldiers in the war zone in Iraq.

Never thought it would actually happen, but I was able to visit one of my dearest friends, J, on her base in Baghdad today. J is my old college roommate who has allowed me to reprint her letters home on this blog to show the evolution of a military mom on her first deployment as a medic in Iraq. (The latest installments—10, 11, 12—are at the bottom of this entry, making for a much longer post than normal.)

My drivers dropped me off at the FOB (forward operating base) at 1 p.m. The FOBs I'm used to are sprawling, air-conditioned American villages with commissaries that look like miniature Wal-Marts, except with an inordinate supply of chewing tobacco and beef jerky. J's FOB, however, is a dusty little outpost sandwiched by forbidding Iraqi installations. Can't say much more about the location, I'm afraid, because my visit was not sanctioned by the military's media coordinators.

My escort truck pulled up with a white South African driver and a uniformed U.S. soldier with sunglasses on in the

Hannah Allam, "June 22 2008: Special Edition: Letters Home 10, 11, 12," *Middle East Diary*, June 22, 2008. Reproduced by permission.

passenger seat. It took me a moment to realize that the soldier was female. Another moment to recognize her as J, a woman I know better in boot-cut jeans and cute tops that show off her dolphin tattoo. I wanted to leap at her, to pull her close and give thanks for this firsthand proof that she was safe. But I could not. There were too many Iraqi police of uncertain loyalties around, and it would have been dangerous for me (and my drivers) if they saw me embrace "an occupier."

Visiting with J

I got a visitor's badge and J showed me to her room, a concrete square with chipped paint on the walls and a huge mass of body armor on the floor. Pictures of J's beautiful 2-year-old daughter hung on a metal locker. Starburst candy and Big Red gum were on top of a file cabinet. Her journal was open on a desk; it's where she writes the letters that eventually end up here.

Alone, we hugged for an eternity, then laughed at how freakin' surreal this whole encounter was. I asked her where we both went wrong in life to end up together in this sunbaked war zone, seemingly a million miles from everything familiar. There was no good answer.

Lounging on her cot, we were just girlfriends again, each of us in our uniforms—hers camouflage, mine the long skirt and modest blouse I wear in an attempt to "blend in" among Iraqis. We sounded so strange and grown-up, discussing how the Mahdi Army [of radical Iraqi cleric Muqtada al-Sadr] had infiltrated the security forces or sharing stories about Sadr City. She said she wanted so badly to forge friendships with her Iraqi comrades, but there was always an insurmountable barrier of mistrust on both sides.

We talked a lot about her marvelous husband, who is doing yeoman's work in the struggle to hold it all together back home, the workaday drudge coupled with round-the-clock, single-parent care of their daughter. I've seen on countless occasions the way this war has ripped apart Iraqi families. When J's eyes grew watery as she described how much she misses her loved ones, I saw for the first time the mirror effect on the families of American troops.

Iraq was new and exciting for her, she said, and the novelty helps the time pass. But what clock is her husband on? How slowly and painfully his days must unfold. J's military stint is almost up and she faces the momentous decision of whether to re-up. The Army is dangling a bonus of $15,000—tax-free—if she renews her contract. J and her husband could use the money, but their daughter could use a mother even more.

Touring the Military Base

We lightened things up by heading over to the chow hall. A kind manager allowed me in even though I was violating the dress code by wearing open-toed shoes. Taco salad! Pecan pie! Sweetened ice tea! Then a walking tour of the base: the latrine where one stall is reserved for Iraqis, the recreation center with an old-timey popcorn machine and a foosball table, barracks where a tongue-in-cheek list was taped to a door under the title "What We're Fighting For." The list included McDonald's, Starbucks, Valium, Republicans, Democrats . . .

And, finally, with the clock running down too quickly, we returned to her room for one last heart-to-heart. The previous occupants had painted a grinning skull on the door, but J's fellow troops decided the old decor wasn't exactly appropriate for a medic. Someone in her unit had dug up a vintage poster of a wartime nurse and stuck it on her door. The caption is: The Comforter.

Letters Home

Below are the latest of J's letters home, which cover everything from good-natured fun with the lonely Iraqi police who approach her with fake stomachaches to J dealing with her rage and fear as she conducts a physical on a suspected insurgent before his interrogation. You can see her trying to make sense of this foreign culture, viewing it through all-American eyes.

I found some of her writings in this installment disturbing, particularly when it comes to torture as an interrogation practice. Doesn't sound like the J I know who volunteered in Haiti. I wonder if this war already has hardened her. But then, in the next sentence, she'll be talking about watching Iraqi children play, or how she wishes she could spend just one day in an Iraqi marketplace. Stereotypes are busted through dialogue and the mingling of peoples. But there's so little of that in this city of fiefdoms divided by nationality or sect.

As usual, only identifying details have been changed. Thanks for your patience with the looong Sunday read.

May 26, 2008

Hello All,

I know I'm still like a month behind in my writings, but hopefully this week I can get caught up.

It's starting to really get warm here, but I know it's not even close to what it will get to in july and august. I did another traffic circle mission on may 22nd but this time I stayed in the vehicle for all of but maybe 1 1/2 hours of a 12 hour mission. I passed out some stuffed animals today and some candy. What amazed me most today is how young the little boys here start womanizing. Boys that seemed only about 9 yrs old would give you a little flirtatious smirk and stare into your eyes until you looked away. They would also smile and give a quick raise of their eyebrows which seems to be quite the popular gesture of flirting here for men and boys of all ages. I know boys start getting interested in females around that age or so, but in America they are not that openly flirtatious so young. I couldn't help but laugh. You will also get the "I'm undressing you with my eyes right now" look by most of the men that pass by and it's a little creepy. You feel like you are up for sale at a market or something. One of the Iraqi Army guys even asked one of the guys I was with if he wanted to take me up stairs and do "freaky-freaky", but he wanted to watch. He also asked how much for me and 10 of his guys. I mean seriously!!! They offered up 4 camels for another female in a different platoon of ours. The blond hair blue eyes are worth a little more here. So anyway, that was a little disturbing.

I visited with my little shop owner friend (Abu Wissam) and we talked about the differences in our cultures . . . here, if necessary, a son may live in his parents' home along with his wife and children, forever. The daughter will move out with her new husband. He also found it odd that women work outside the home in America and that sometimes the men stay at home. He gasped at this and said here, that would be a total disgrace of a man to stay home with the children.

He also said that Baghdad used to be a very beautiful place to live. But now you can't go out at night because it is too dangerous. He said when Saddam [Hussein, the deposed dictator,] ran things you didn't have a voice, but it was safe and you could go to the casinos at night or out to eat. Now you have a voice, but it's too dangerous with all the militia, criminals, etc. Men here can have up to 4 wives, but he said that it is difficult to have that many unless you have a lot of money. He also asked where I was from and I explained to him our type of weather. He said this weather right now (100–105) was spring to him, but july and august are almost intolerable. If the locals can't even stand it, how are we supposed to?

Next, he asked if there are Indians where I live, like the ones he's seen in the movies with big feathers and stuff. And he said, "You know, the ones that go 'hiyah, hiyah'" (and he put his hand up to his mouth). I thought that was so cute. But I had to break it to him that they don't live in teepees anymore. I told him that they live in regular houses, dress like us and drive cars. He looked very intrigued by this and almost disappointed. I tried to explain that I was part Indian, but I don't think he grasped it.

May 25th

We had a mass casualty drill today on the FOB. This is where they simulate a mortar coming in or something like that and have a bunch of pretend injuries. So when the sirens went off, all of the medical personnel ran to the aid station and started "working" on patients and evacuating them by helicopter. It was a good experience and things get really hectic and loud when you have 30 patients at one time show up. I can only imagine how much worse it would be if it was real. We did actually have 2 real life injuries though. A ceiling fan flew off and hit a girl in the head (cutting it open) and a guy right under the nose (he had to have stitches and there was blood everywhere). That added a little excitement to the night.

The other day while one of my medics was on mission, a convoy stopped and a sergeant major [SGM] walked over to where they were standing. This particular medic doesn't like to follow many rules and so he was not wearing his gloves or eye protection. He is also Korean. So, the SGM walks up looks at him and then goes over to our other guys and asks if that guy, V, is our interpreter. They said no, he's part of our company. Then the SGM walks over to him and asks why the hell he isn't wearing all of his gear. Sooooo, V, being offended and being the smart ass he is says "Me no speaka English". Too freakin hillarious!!! Needless to say he got his ass chewed, but I still have to give him credit for being so ballzy.

Gotta cruise for now, sorry this one is kind of short. Love and miss you all,

J

May 26, 2008

Today was my first time out to an Iraqi police [IP] station. Most of our squads are in charge of certain police stations and go out everyday to make sure they are doing their job, show them how to do certain things, and fix any problems they might have. Some police stations are better than others, of course, and some of them are mostly infiltrated by the militia so you really can't trust anyone here.

The Iraqi General of this station likes to have his blood pressure checked everyday and also his blood sugar (like it's going to make a difference, they don't do anything about it anyway), but anyway we do this to appease them. Win their hearts and minds. That's what the slogan for the war is now. I am the first female to be at this station, so of course I get the stare down and all the eyebrow raises I could want. No one knew I was the medic, because once they know that, it would be all over for me.

It was fairly nice in there. Nice and air-conditioned, we were able to sit on nice comfortable faux leather couches, and were served tea. All tea over here, no matter what the flavor, is called chai. So I just sat there and watched TV while the squad leaders did their normal routine of finding out if there's been any crime in the last 24 hours, if everyone is showing up for work, if the vehicles are getting fixed, if the weapons work, if they are wearing their uniforms, etc. (again just babysitting them). So after an hour or so we went upstairs to the general's office. The squad leaders did their thing and then they told him I was there to do his BP [blood pressure] and blood sugar. I did what I had to do, we had some more tea, and then were supposed to go home. Just as we were leaving they received info that 2 different people could be served warrants today for possibly being involved with aiding an escapee from a hospital that was wanted for murder. So we went out with the IP squad and snuck up on two different houses and got the people we needed. Almost everyone stayed in their vehicles, only a few dismounted. I unfortunately couldn't even see anything because they put the medic in the safest vehicle (ASV) [armored security vehicle] and you are way in the back with a window about 8x3inches. I had to count on the gunner to give me a play by play. So anyway, we took the 2 detainees back to the station and then headed back home.

The next day we went back to the same station. We sat there, drank tea, chit-chatted (this totally beats sitting in the humvee all cramped up by the way) and then I did the usual on the general. My commander then had me look at a little boy (kids can come to work with their parents sometimes) that was complaining of pain below the knee, worse in the morning and got better throughout the day. There was no swelling or injury associated with it so I'm assuming it was Osgood Schlatters [disease; childhood inflammation of the knee joint], but couldn't be sure so just gave them some children's aspirin and told them he would probably outgrow it, but to see a doc if it gets worse. At this point the word started to spread that I was a medic, although here they just call you doctor.

Turns out the woman that was detained yesterday was breast feeding so she had to bring her baby with her to jail. Interesting. There was also another woman in there along with her husband. Her father had them arrested because they got married without his approval of the man. She was going to be released later that day because I guess they worked things out. What a crappy way of life for a woman over here. I'm so thankful for all of the women in the past that worked so hard to get equality for women [in the West].

I then was asked to look at a detainee who was stabbed and had stitches. While doing this, all the other detainees gathered around and stared at me like I was a zoo animal. A little weird at first, but then I got used to it. It looked fine, but possibly getting a little infected on one edge so I just gave him some ointment and rewrapped it for him. However, before doing this, I thought I might have a little fun with them. So I told the class clown IP of the station to tell him in Arabic that it's not good, we're going to have to cut it off. The IP tried not to smile, so he must have known I was joking, he told the guy (whose eyes got really big) and then the IP said to me, "you are just joking, right?" I said yes, and then he told him truth and they all started to laugh and the detainee looked very relieved. I know, a little evil, but fun. At this point I knew there was no turning back. They all knew now for sure I was the medic, so I knew it was only a matter of time before the fake sicknesses began.

Well, sure enough, about 10 minutes later the one IP came and got me because I need to look at Capt. Mohammed. I was told he is not feeling well (even though I saw him perfectly fine just awhile ago). So I walk in to the room (which is filled with about 6 other IP's watching) and he is lying on his bed, holding his stomach, and is trying to look like he is in great pain. He is a horrible actor by the way. So I humored him and did a quick set of vitals and an overall assessment. He said he had stomach pains and diarrhea. I told the terp (interpreter) to tell him that I think he is pregnant. The terp said "do you really want me to tell him that?", and I said of course! So he told him in Arabic that he was going to have a baby and the room erupted in laughter. [Then] N (the goofball of the bunch who can also speak English very well) shouted, "Congratulations! It's a girl!" The IP's got a kick out of this too and everyone was laughing. I then gave Mohammed some Rolaids just to settle his stomach if he really was having issues and N chimes in again and says "I know what those are for. Those are for his period." At this point Capt Mohammed was not living this episode down and everyone was stopping in to see what the laughter was all about. It was a good time. It was great to see that they have a sense of humor just like us and that we are all not so different from one another.

Before I left the room one of the younger IP's stopped me and said, with a smile on his face, "We are all sick here". "I'm sure you are", I replied. I really enjoyed going to this station. It's way better than being out on a traffic control point where you don't really get to interact with very many people. Also, it's nice because this particular station is really clean compared to most, that's what they tell me anyway. Even the detainee cell (which I was expecting to look like a Mexican prison cell or my first room) was clean and the detainees even looked unusually upbeat for being in jail. I saw a few women walk by and asked about them. I was told that they now hire a few female police to search and also take care of the female detainees.

For lunch we ate some Iraqi bread called samun and had a cheese spread with it called jibbin. It was sooo good. It's a good thing I don't come here everyday because the warm fresh bread and cheese on top could really do some damage to all the running I've been doing. Well, I think I've rambled on enough for now. Much love to you all.

Love,

J

A Journalist Travels Inside Iraq

Michael Massing

Journalist Michael Massing in the following piece writes about his visit to the front line of the Iraq War. While Massing believes that many members of the U.S. military express candid opinions about the war, he worries that many Iraqis will not feel as free to speak openly. But even while U.S. soldiers talk enthusiastically about the help they are providing in Iraq, he notes they are less willing to discuss mistakes that have been made. Although visiting the front line in Iraq with U.S. troops provides media access, Massing argues that this access may be one-sided, blinding journalists to the complete story of the Iraq War.

Over the last five years [2003–2008], as I've consumed one dispatch after another from journalists embedded with U.S. soldiers in Iraq, I've wondered how accurate a picture of events such reports provide. Given the stark dangers journalists face in Iraq, embedding clearly offers a valuable means of getting around the country and seeing the troops in action—but at what cost? Does the presence of journalists affect the way soldiers behave? Do journalists—physically protected by soldiers—in turn protect them in what they choose to write? How willing are soldiers to talk freely about their experiences? And to what extent is it possible to talk with Iraqis while on an embed?

This past May [2008], on a visit to Baghdad, I got a chance to explore such questions myself. On my embed application, I wrote that I wanted to visit a typical Baghdad neighborhood to see the effects of the surge [troop increase] and to get an

Michael Massing, "Blind Spot: Seeing Iraq Through Uncle Sam's Eyes," *Columbia Journalism Review*, vol. 47, September-October, 2008, pp. 14–16. Copyright © 2008 Columbia Journalism Review. Reproduced by permission of the publisher and the author.

idea of what more had to be done before the U.S. could begin to reduce its forces in significant numbers. I was assigned to the Second Battalion of the Fourth Infantry Regiment of the Tenth Mountain Division, a light infantry unit stationed in the southern Baghdad neighborhood of Dora.

Talking with American Soldiers

At 9 o'clock on a blistering morning in mid-May, I was met in the Green Zone by a four-vehicle military convoy. Emerging to introduce themselves were Lieutenant Colonel Timothy Watson, the battalion's commanding officer, and Captain Brett Walker, the public-affairs officer (PAO) assigned to watch over me. On the fifteen-minute ride to Dora, they told me how a year earlier the neighborhood had been one of the most violent in Baghdad, with Sunni fighters attached to Al Qaeda in Iraq setting off car bombs and leaving mutilated bodies along roadsides. But thanks in part to the stationing of hundreds more troops in the area, to the application of counterinsurgency techniques, and to the Sunni insurgents who had turned against Al Qaeda, Dora had become one of the safest districts in Baghdad. The Dora marketplace, which the previous year had been all but shuttered, was once again thriving, with some eight hundred shops and stalls open for business.

In the marketplace, I was met by an infantry patrol and taken on a walk-through. Over the next twelve hours, I would see a local church that had recently reopened; a joint security station where both U.S. and Iraqi soldiers were based, and where I could talk with some American troops; a school that the U.S. had helped to refurbish; another, smaller marketplace, where we encountered three "Sons of Iraq"—former insurgents now working with the U.S.; a house that U.S. soldiers had blown up after discovering bomb-making materials inside; and Forward Operation Base Falcon, a sprawling U.S. camp in southern Baghdad.

Though brief, my embed put to rest some of my concerns about the process. To begin, it dispelled any doubts I had about the willingness of soldiers to speak candidly. Several mid-level officers complained vigorously to me about the multiple deployments they'd been on. Some had been to Iraq and Afghanistan three, four, even five times, and their relationships at home had suffered. One captain told me that he had been stop-lossed [given an involuntary extension of duty]; another said that he had stayed on only because he knew he would be stop-lossed if he tried to leave. A military-intelligence officer spoke on the record about what he saw as the weaknesses in U.S. strategy. While the surge had helped to bring Al Qaeda under control, Staff Sergeant Zachery Brown told me, the U.S. still needed to deal with Iraq's many political and social problems and, as far as he could see, it lacked a coherent policy for doing so.

Not every soldier I met felt aggrieved, of course. Some expressed satisfaction at the help they felt they were providing to Iraqis. Others seemed guarded, making it hard to get a fix on their true views; had I spent more time with them, they might have opened up more. All in all, I came away convinced that embedding provides an excellent opportunity for journalists to talk with soldiers, see them in action, and get a sense of how they see their work.

Talking with Iraqis

Talking to Iraqis is another matter. I had a few chances to approach the locals, but these tended to be fleeting and awkward, and my lack of Arabic aggravated the problem. In the Dora marketplace, the soldiers accompanying me spoke expansively about all the microgrants and other assistance they were providing shopkeepers. Yet the shopkeepers kept to themselves, and neither they nor their customers even made eye contact with the soldiers. What, I wondered, was going through their minds? I had no real way of finding out.

Later, when we came upon the three Sons of Iraq, Captain Walker—seeing my interest in interviewing them—moved off so that they could speak without inhibition. An Army interpreter (an Iraqi who wore a ski mask to conceal his identity) remained by my side. The three Sons, in tattered beige uniforms, seemed eager to talk. Dora, they said, "had died" while in Al Qaeda's grip, but now "everything has changed." The Americans, they added, "are doing good things."

What more, I asked, remained to be done? Providing jobs, they replied. One of the men pointed to a row of half-finished buildings across the way. Three hundred people could be put to work completing them, he said, but the Iraqi government had little interest in helping out—it was "too sectarian." I couldn't tell if this last remark came from the interpreter or from the Sons. The interpreter's next comment—"Every house we're in, the people say, 'Can you help us?'"—clearly came from him, and as the interview wound on, it became increasingly hard for me to tell where the Sons' views left off and the interpreter's began. Even if the interpreter had been more careful, I'm not sure how much I would have learned, for interviewing former insurgents while surrounded by U.S. troops (within earshot or not) hardly seemed conducive to getting at their true thoughts.

American Aid in Iraq

My inability to talk frankly with Iraqis was all the more frustrating given the many comments the Americans were making about them. The soldiers never said anything overtly negative. They made no references to hajjis or towel-heads. Rather, they spoke incessantly about how much help they were providing the Iraqis. On the ride down to Dora, for instance, Lieutenant Colonel Watson told me how hard the U.S. military was working to boost the capacity of the local government. With violence down, he said, it was essential that the delivery of basic services be improved, and he and his soldiers were straining to figure out the lines of authority among various Iraqi agencies and to get them to work together. He told me of the satisfaction he felt when the local municipality picked up the trash in the Dora marketplace. "We consider it a huge success when we get the Iraqis to do the job themselves," he said.

At Forward Operating Base Falcon, Captain Emiliano Tellado, a field-artillery officer turned government-fix-it man, told me with great enthusiasm about all the work he was doing with neighborhood councils to streamline the delivery of services. He spoke with pride about how his unit had helped open the first bank in the area and how it was trying to find ways to help the Iraqis improve the pickup of trash, the control of sewage, and the supply of electricity. The Iraqi government, the captain said, "is making a lot of strides."

And so it went throughout my embed. The overall impression conveyed was one of American know-how, expertise, and efficiency and of Iraqi bumbling, idleness, and ineptitude. And, without quite realizing it, I absorbed this perspective. The Iraqi government is almost universally loathed for its disorganization and dysfunctionality, and the soldiers' earnest descriptions of their efforts to mend it jibed with my own preconceived ideas about American competence and can-do spirit.

U.S. Mistakes in Iraq

It was only the day after my embed, while I was interviewing American officials in the Green Zone, that I had a chance to reflect on what I had heard and to place it in broader context. I recalled the nonstop looting that had occurred in the wake of the invasion, a spasm of anarchy that had resulted in the razing of eighteen of twenty-three government ministries. I recollected the de-Baathification order that had been issued by the Coalition Provisional Authority, a sweeping and (most now agree) disastrously ill-conceived decree that had resulted in the dismissal of 120,000 officials, bureaucrats, and civil servants. And I thought about the acute security vacuum that had opened up on the Americans' watch, a catastrophic break-down in authority that had resulted in the slaughter or flight of virtually the entire Iraqi professional and technocratic class. To the extent that Iraq was broken, the U.S.'s many missteps were certainly a major factor.

Nor is such blundering a thing of the past. As I learned during my stay, the U.S., along with its military surge, has carried on a political surge, bringing to Iraq hundreds of advisers, specialists, and contractors to help boost the capacity of Iraqi ministries and improve the quality of services. From conversations I had after my return to the U.S. with two advisers who travel frequently to Iraq, I learned that this project has been a fiasco, with the visitors having few language skills and even less familiarity with how Iraq works. One think-tank analyst who has spent time in Iraq's ministries told me that the Iraqis he met seemed much more capable and knowledgeable than the Americans sent to help them. The U.S., he said, still seemed to be trying to remake Iraq along American-style free-market lines, without much regard for Iraq's history and traditions.

This ran completely counter to assessments I'd heard—and reflexively accepted—during my embed. Enveloped in the cocoon of the U.S. military, exposed nonstop to its views, insulated from independent Iraqi voices, I had bought the storyline—talented, high-minded Americans helping out hapless, pitiable Iraqis—when the truth was far more complicated.

The American Narrative

From conversations I've had with other journalists in Iraq, I know that they take steps to avoid falling into this trap. Leila Fadel of *McClatchy* [news service] (who speaks Arabic) told me that she makes a point of getting the cell phone numbers of Iraqis she encounters on embeds so she can call them afterward and check her impressions with them. Tina Susman of the *Los Angeles Times* told me that, after doing an embed, she sometimes sends an Iraqi reporter back to the site to talk with locals and get their perspectives. Occasionally, U.S. reporters bring along their own interpreters, thus facilitating contact with Iraqis.

No matter what precautions they take, however, it seems to me difficult for U.S. reporters on embeds to avoid getting swept up in the American narrative. As Americans, we come out of the same culture as U.S. soldiers, subscribe to similar values, and bring to foreign societies many of the same preconceptions. As a result, we see the war zone through the eyes of the occupier rather than those of the occupied. And the coverage itself inevitably reflects this, taking on the paternalistic tint that the act of occupation invariably breeds. That this process occurs so subtly and unconsciously makes it all the more dangerous.

Living Inside a War Zone

Riverbend

In this selection, an anonymous female writer relays her experiences with everyday life in war-torn Iraq. She discusses her anger with President Bush's claim that things are getting better in Iraq. She accuses U.S. troops of damaging and burning innocent families' homes and expresses her fatigue over the stresses of everyday life, filled with explosions and often lacking in electricity.

Tuesday, November 18, 2003

DIFFICULT DAYS . . .

They've been bombing houses in Tikrit and other areas! Unbelievable . . . I'm so angry it makes me want to break something!!!! What the hell is going on?! What do the Americans think Tikrit is?! Some sort of city of monsters or beasts? The people there are simple people. Most of them make a living off of their land and their livestock—the rest are teachers, professors and merchants—they have lives and families . . . Tikrit is nothing more than a bunch of low buildings and a palace that was as inaccessible to the Tikritis as it was to everyone else!

People in Al Awja suffered as much as anyone, if not more—they weren't all related to Saddam and even those who were suffered under his direct relatives. Granted, his bodyguards and others close to him were from Tikrit, but they aren't currently in Tikrit—the majority have struck up deals with the CPA [Coalition Provisional Authority] and are bargaining for their safety and the safety of their families with information. The people currently in Tikrit are just ordinary people whose homes and children are as precious to them as American homes and children are precious to Americans! This is contemptible and everyone thinks so—Sunnis and Shi'a alike are shaking their heads incredulously.

And NO—I'm not Tikriti—I'm not even from the "triangle"—but I know simple, decent people who ARE from there and just the thought that this is being done is so outrageous it makes me want to scream. How can that ass of a president say things are getting better in Iraq when his troops have stooped to destroying homes?! Is that a sign that things are getting better? When you destroy someone's home and detain their family, why would they want to go on with life? Why wouldn't they want to lob a bomb at some 19-year-old soldier from Missouri?!

The Troops

The troops were pushing women and children shivering with fear out the door in the middle of the night. What do you think these children think to themselves—being dragged out of their homes, having their possessions and houses damaged and burned?! Who do you think is creating the "terrorists"?!! Do you think these kids think to themselves, "Oh well—we learned our lesson. That's that. Yay troops!" It's like a vicious, moronic circle and people are outraged. . . .

The troops are claiming that the attacks originate from these areas—the people in the areas claim the attacks are coming from somewhere else. . . . I really am frightened of what this is going to turn into. People seem to think that Iraq is broken into zones and areas—ethnically and religiously divided. That's just not true—the majority of people have relatives all over Iraq. My relatives extend from Mosul all the way down to Basrah—we all feel for each other and it makes decent people crazy to see this happening.

There have also been a string of raids all over Baghdad, but especially in Al-A'adhamiya. They've detained dozens of people with the excuse that they own more than one weapon. Who owns less than two weapons? Everyone has at least one Klashnikov and a couple of guns. Every male in the house is usually armed and sometimes the females are too. It's not because we love turning our homes into arsenals, but because the situation was so dangerous (and in some areas still is) that no one wants to take any risks. Imagine the scene: a blue mini-van pulls up ... 10 dirty, long-haired men clamber out with Klashnikovs, pistols and grenades and demand all the gold and the kids (for ransom). Now imagine trying to face them all with a single handgun ... if Baghdad were SECURE people would give up their weapons. I hate having weapons in the house.

I'm so tired. These last few days have been a strain on every single nerve in my body. The electricity has been out for the last three days and while the weather is pleasant it really is depressing.

This Feels Like War

No one knows why the electricity is out—there are murmurings of storms and damage to generators and sabotage and punishment ... no one knows exactly what's going on. There are explosions everywhere. Yesterday it was especially heavy. Today there was a huge explosion that felt like it was nearby but we can't really tell. How do you define a war? This sure as hell feels like war to me ... no electricity, water at a trickle, planes, helicopters and explosions.

We didn't send the kids to school today. My cousin's wife spent last night talking about horrible premonitions and it didn't take much to convince my cousin that they would be better off at home.

It's hard for adults without electricity, but it's a torment for the kids. They refuse to leave the little pool of light provided by the kerosene lamps. We watch them nervously as they flit from candle-light to lamplight, trying to avoid the dark as much as possible. I have flashes of the children knocking down a candle, hot, burning wax, flames . . . I asked the 7-year-old the other night if she was afraid of "monsters" when she shied away from a dark room. She looked at me like I was crazy—monsters are for losers who don't need to fear war, abductions and explosions.

We (5 houses in the neighborhood) all chipped in and bought a generator immediately after the war. What we do now is 2 houses get enough electricity for some neon lights, a television, a refrigerator and a freezer. We asked them to "save our electricity up" and give us a couple of hours after futtoor and that's how I'm typing now. But my time is almost up and I'm afraid if the electricity goes off suddenly, it'll damage my computer.

Appreciating Light

E. and I hang out on the roof after futtoor and only duck inside when the helicopters begin hovering above. We watch the main street from the roof. One of the merchants has a little generator and he sets up chairs outside of his shop, in front of a small black and white tv. The guys in the neighborhood all stream towards the lights like ants towards a sticky spot. They sit around drinking tea and chatting.

You really can't appreciate light until you look down upon a blackened city and your eyes are automatically drawn to the pinpoints of brightness provided by generators . . . it looks like the heavens have fallen and the stars are wandering the streets of Baghdad, lost and alone.

I have to go now. Hope the electricity is back tomorrow, at least.

CHAPTER 2

The American Home Front

Balancing Family and Military Service

Anthony Agee

A career U.S. Army sergeant discusses in the following article the difficulty of balancing his military life with his home life. When his kids were younger, he remembers, it was easier; now, during his third deployment to Iraq, his kids are beginning to ask why he has to be away from home. He also realizes that being away from home places a larger burden on his wife, who oversees the daily needs of the children. Long deployments, he realizes, can place a lot of stress on marriages.

I was born and raised in Clanton, Alabama. I am the oldest of seven kids. My father is prior military also—he's a veteran of the Vietnam War.

I saw what the military did for my father as far as being able to come in the military, have a career, and then after five to six years, he got out of the military and started his own business. Initially, that was my plan also. . . . But after I was in the military for four years, I decided to re-enlist for another two to three years to continue with my military career. I realized it was something I really wanted to do.

I enjoy what I do in the military—lead soldiers, train them, mentor them—but I also understand that there's a cost [to] my family. My deployments to OIF-1, -3, and -5, those are a year [each]. When I talk with my kids now, they'll try to remind me of something that happened during that time-frame and then they'll say, "Oh, you were deployed during that time, you wouldn't remember it." I know I'll never get that time back.

Balancing Two Lives

I'm a soldier first; I'm a dad first, also, and I have to balance that.

My kids are getting older now to where they're starting to understand what's going on in the world a little bit more, and they're starting to ask more and more questions: where I'm going, what I do when I get there, what's it like, do I have to do certain things. It's a challenge to try to put things in perspective for them.

If you ask do I think it's worth it, yes I do, because I would rather go through things that I'm going through now to prevent my sons from having to face the same challenges and same threats in the world that we're currently facing.

[Between the second and third deployments to Iraq], there was a nine-month gap. That was a big challenge.

We knew before we redeployed [back to the United States] that we would be back in nine months. Initially, morale was kind of down, because the soldiers [were] looking forward to getting back, spending some time with their family. That nine-month gap don't give you a lot of time to get reacquainted.

For my 4-year-old, it's over 50 percent [of her life that I've been deployed]. When I left to deploy, she was 4 months old, almost 5 months old. When I came back, she was almost a year and a half; and then I left again for another year.

When I was younger, I wanted to deploy; it didn't bother me, faze me, as far as being away from my family. The older I've become and the longer I've been in, I guess I've become a little wiser and I've seen the second- and third-order effects that it has.

It's kind of sad when you see the kids crying and your wife crying and you've got to tell them, hey, I'll be back in a year. That's the challenging part. I try to prep them and make them understand that this is something that I choose to do, because we all have a choice—I could easily get out of the military—but trying to make them understand that we have to sacrifice something. And I'm not saying that I'm willing to sacrifice my family, but with every sacrifice comes a great gain. I do it so hopefully they won't have to do it in the years to come. . . .

Home Life Without Dad

My 10-year-old, he says ["let someone else go"] all the time. He says, "You just did it, it's somebody else's turn." He doesn't understand.

The challenge in my field is there's not that many of us to actually rotate. That's why we end up being in that nine-month turn, because there's a requirement out there for Afghanistan, Iraq, for engineers, specifically the field of engineers that I'm in.

Sometimes kids act out when they're away from their family. It affects kids and people in different ways. My son, he's become more conscious of what's going on in the world, so he tries to watch the news a lot, see what's going on. And during that time he was only like 7, 8 years old, and that's too young for him to be worrying about things that are going on in the world. But in his eyes he's got a vested interest in it because I'm involved.

[For] my wife [who is herself an army veteran], who's used to having a partner to share with some of the duties around the house and helping out with the kids, a sounding board for her, now that's taken out of the equation—that's more stressful for her.

That was a real big challenge for both me and my spouse; but after OIF-1 [in 2003–2004], my wife got out [of the army] to give a little stability to our kids and keep the home front stable. She had been in for 12 years, so it was kind of hard for her to just throw 12 years away. But with the constant deployment cycle and the optempo [operational tempo], we had to make a decision, and the family needed one of us there, and with me being the senior ranking [soldier] and being in longer, she decided to go ahead and get out.

Military Marriages

I have a lot of respect for military wives and spouses because they shoulder a lot when their other half is actually gone. A lot of them, it's their first time, because you've got a lot of young couples out there that's not used to being separated for an extended period of time from their loved ones, and they do a phenomenal job shouldering the burden.

I was stressing to those guys [in my unit about] all of the resource agencies that are out there for soldiers to take advantage of, to try to get their significant other or their spouse incorporated into the Family Readiness Groups that are back here, to take advantage of the Army OneSource (www.armyone source.com) counseling that's available to soldiers and their families.

There are couples out there that fight through it, they weather that storm, and their marriage is just as strong as ever. I've been fortunate to have a supportive wife that's been there by my side. That gives me a peace of mind and the flexibility to be able to share positive experiences with my soldiers and tell them, me and my wife, we're going through it too, and I'm in the same boat as you are, and we're dealing with it, and we're making it.

My Son Is a Soldier in Iraq

Teri Wills Allison

In the following selection, Teri Wills Allison—a soldier's mother—talks about the emotional strain of having a son who is deployed in Iraq. First, Allison explains, there is the challenge of living every day with dread and despair, along with the strain on family ties over the justness of the war in Iraq. She realizes that her emotional pain, however, does not compare to the real-life injuries and deaths suffered by both Americans and Iraqis during the war. Allison has also seen the aftermath of the war up close, she relates, when visiting her son's friends who have returned from Iraq with emotional and physical scars. While she confesses that many soldiers' mothers may not agree with her views, she continues to believe that the Iraq War is built on lies.

I am not a pacifist. I am a mother. By nature, the two are incompatible, for even a cottontail rabbit will fight to protect her young. Violent action may well be necessary in defense of one's family or home (and that definition of home can easily be extended to community and beyond); but violence, no matter how warranted, always takes a heavy toll. And violence taken to the extreme—war—exacts the most extreme costs. A just war there may be, but there is no such thing as a good war. And the burdens of an unjust war are insufferable.

I know something about the costs of an unjust war, for my son, Nick—an infantryman in the U.S. Army—is fighting one in Iraq. I don't speak for my son. I couldn't even if I wanted to, for all I hear through the Mom Filter is: "I'm fine, Mom, don't worry, I'm fine, everything is fine, fine, fine, we're fine, just fine." But I can tell you what some of the costs are as I live and breathe them.

Everyday Problems

First, the minor stuff: my constant feelings of dread and de-spair; the sweeping rage that alternates with petrifying fear; the torrents of tears that accompany a maddening sense of helplessness and vulnerability. My son is involved in a deadly situation that should never have been. I feel like a mother lion in a cage, my grown cub in danger, and all I can do is throw myself furiously against the bars, impotent to protect him. My tolerance for bullshit is zero, and I've snapped off more heads in the last several months than in all my 48 years combined.

For the first time in my life, and with great amazement and sorrow, I feel what can only be described as hatred. It took me a long time to admit it, but there it is. I loathe the hubris, the callousness, and the lies of those in the [George W.] Bush administration who led us into this war. Truth be told, I even loathe the fallible and very human purveyors of those lies. I feel no satisfaction in this admission, only sadness and recognition. And hope that—given time—I can do better. I never wanted to hate anyone.

[The antianxiety medicine] Xanax helps a bit. At least it holds the debilitating panic attacks somewhat at bay, so I can fake it through one more day. A friend in the same situation relies on a six pack of beer every night; another has drifted into a la-la land of denial. Nice.

Then there is the wedge that's been driven between part of my extended family and me. They don't see this war as one based on lies. They've become evangelical believers in a false faith, swallowing Bush's fear mongering, his chicken-hawk posturing and strutting, and cheering his "bring 'em on" atti-tude as a sign of strength and resoluteness. Perhaps life is just easier that way. These are the same people who have known my son since he was a baby, who have held him and loved him and played with him, who have bought him birthday pre-sents and taken him fishing. I don't know them anymore.

American and Iraq Casualties

But enough of my whining. My son is alive and in one piece, unlike the 1,102 dead and 7,782 severely wounded American soldiers; which equals 8,884 blood soaked uniforms, and doesn't even count the estimated 20,000 troops—not publicly reported by the Department of Defense—medivaced out of Iraq for "non-combat related injuries." Every death, every injury burns like a knife in my gut, for these are all America's sons and daughters. And I know I'm not immune to that knock on my door [announcing my son's been killed] either.

And what of the Iraqi people? How many casualties have they suffered? How many tens of thousands dead and wounded? How many Iraqi mothers have wept, weep now, for their lost children? I fear we will never know, for though the Pentagon has begun—almost gleefully—counting Iraqi insurgent deaths, there is little chance of getting an accurate verification of civilian casualties. You know, "collateral damage."

Yes, my son is alive and, as far as I know, well. I wish I could say the same for some of his friends.

The Aftermath of War

One young man who was involved in heavy fighting during the invasion is now so debilitated by post-traumatic stress disorder [PTSD] that he routinely has flashbacks in which he smells burning flesh; he can't close his eyes without seeing people's heads squashed like frogs in the middle of the road, or dead and dying women and children, burned, bleeding and dismembered. Sometimes he hears the sounds of battle raging around him, and he has been hospitalized twice for suicidal tendencies. When he was home on leave, this 27 year old man would crawl into his mother's room at night and sob in her lap for hours. Instead of getting treatment for PTSD, he has just received a "less than honorable" discharge from the Army. The rest of his unit redeploys to Iraq in [a few months].

Another friend of Nick's was horrifically wounded when his Humvee stopped on an IED [improvised explosive device]. He didn't even have time to instinctively raise his arm and protect his face. Shrapnel ripped through his right eye, obliterating it to gooey shreds, and penetrated his brain. He has been in a coma [for seven months]. His mother spends every day with him in the hospital; his wife is devastated, and their 1 1/2 year old daughter doesn't know her daddy. But my son's friend is a fighter and so is making steady, incremental progress toward consciousness. He has a long hard struggle ahead of him, one that he need never have faced—and his family has had to fight every step of the way to get him the treatment he needs. So much for supporting the troops.

I go visit him every week and it breaks my heart to see the burned faces, the missing limbs, the limps, the vacant stares one encounters in an acute-care military hospital. In front of the hospital there is a cannon, and every afternoon they blast that sucker off. You should see all the poor guys hit the pavement. Though many requests have been made to discontinue the practice for the sake of the returning wounded, the general in charge refuses. Boom.

Then there is Nick's 24 year old Kurdish friend, the college-educated son of teachers, multilingual and highly intelligent. He works as a translator for the U.S. Army for $600 a month and lives on base, where he is relatively safe. (Translators for private contractors, also living on base, make $7200 a month). He wants to travel to the States to continue his education, but no visas are now being issued from Iraq. Once the army is through with him, will they just send him back into the streets, a virtual dead man for having worked with the Americans? My son places a high premium on loyalty to family and friends, and he has been raised to walk his talk. This must be a harsh and embittering lesson on just how unprincipled the rest of the world can be. My heart aches for his Iraqi friend as well as for him.

Life as a Military Mom

When Nick left for Iraq, I granted myself permission to be stark raving mad for the length of his deployment. By god, I've done a good job of it, without apology or excuse. And I dare say there are at least 139,999 other moms who have done the same—though taking troop rotations into consideration to maintain that magical number of 140,000 in the sand could put the number of crazed military moms as high as 300,000, maybe more. Right now, you might want to be careful about cutting in line in front of a middle-aged woman.

I know there are military moms who view the war in Iraq through different ideological lenses than mine. Sometimes I envy them. God, how much easier it must be to believe one's son or daughter is fighting for a just and noble cause! But no matter how hard I scrutinize the invasion and occupation of Iraq, all I see are lies, corruption, and greed fueled by a powerful addiction to oil. Real soldiers get blown to tatters in their "Hummers," so that well-heeled American suburbanites can play in theirs.

For my family and me, the costs of this war are real and not abstract. By day, I fight my demons of dreaded possibility, beat them back into the shadows, into the dark recesses of my mind. Every night, they hiss and whisper a vile prognosis of gloom and desolation. I order the voices into silence, but too often they laugh at and mock my commands.

I wonder if George Bush ever hears these voices.

And I wonder, too just how much are we willing to pay for a gallon of gas?

The Everyday Life of Iraq War Veterans

Colby Buzzell

In the following essay, Colby Buzzell explains the direction that his and a number of his friends' lives have taken after returning from military service in Iraq. As he meets old friends from his pre-army days, he realizes he no longer has anything in common with them; as he reunites with army friends, however, he watches them struggle and readjust to civilian life. While one of his friends gets married and attempts to start a "normal" life, most of his army buddies are drifting from day to day, trying to find jobs and rebuild their lives. Because of the difficulty of this, he realizes, many of his friends eventually re-enlist in the military.

A couple months before this story starts, I went back home and met up with a few of my civilian friends for some beers at a bar we used to all hang out at. It was good to see them all again, since I hadn't seen them in years and had no idea what any of them have been up to, and my one friend then told me, "I just want to let you know that I don't support the war, and I think the whole thing is just bullshit, but I'm glad you made it back."

So I thanked him, not really sure if that was a compliment or not, and he then went on to say that he thinks all this "Support the troops" stuff is just a bunch of flag-waving bullshit and that there needs to be more pressure on the troops to end this war. Confused, I asked him what he meant by that, and he told me that the reason why the Vietnam War ended is that people protested the troops as well as the war, and we need to do the same thing now, because the troops are just as

Colby Buzzell, "The Best Years of Our Lives: Every Generation Has Its War Veterans," *Esquire*, vol. 145, March, 2006, pp. 206–14. Copyright 2006 by Colby Buzzell for *Esquire*. Reproduced by permission of International Creative Management, Inc.

responsible as the politicians, and they don't have to fight if they don't want to. I told him it's not as easy as that, then I jokingly asked him, "Well, what do you mean, do you think we should be spitting on the troops when they get back or what?"

He thought about that one for a second, said, "Well . . ." and looked up at me with his nodding head, and said, "Yeah."

I finished my beer, told them that it was good to see all of them again, but I had to leave, and so I did. And I realized that whatever friends I had before the Army no longer really exist. The only friends that I have now are the ones I made while I was in.

Army Friends

Haji[1] don't surf, and I didn't think Callahan did either until I visited him down in San Diego, where he was living with Vance. Callahan's decision to move to southern California was actually made up in a guard tower back in Mosul, Iraq, where we'd been stationed together, bringing righteousness to that land. . . .

The last time I saw Vance and Callahan, we were at a bar in Olympia, Washington, not far from Fort Lewis, where we were stationed. It was the night before my last day in the Army. I remember that night as being somewhat depressing. Horrocks, Cannon, Vance, Callahan, and a couple other close friends of mine from the platoon were all there, and I knew that it could be the last time I ever saw them. I wondered about that for a while. Some of them still had years left on their military contracts, some reenlisted, and some got out. I was one that got out. A few months later, Vance and Callahan both transitioned out of the Army as well.

1. *Haji* is a title or form of address for a Muslim who has made the pilgrimage (Hajj) to Mecca, as required by Islamic law. It has become a somewhat derogatory reference for Iraqi Muslims used by American soldiers in Iraq, similar to the name "Charlie" used by American GIs during the Vietnam War in reference to the Vietnamese. The author here makes a reference to the Vietnam War movie *Apocalypse Now* where one air cavalry commander comments, "Charlie don't surf."

In Mosul, they were in the same line squad, and they'd also been stationed in Germany together; because of this, they would always pair up on force protection in the guard towers. They'd spend countless hours chain-smoking Haji cigarettes, staring off into the Mosul skyline, talking about their plans once deployment ended and they were out. Vance was looking forward to going back home to sunny San Diego, and he'd tell Callahan, who had never been to California before, all about it—the beaches, the surf, the food, the bars, the women, the laid-back California attitude, etc. Callahan wasn't really sure what he wanted to do once he got out, so Vance suggested that he come visit San Diego and stay at his mom's place for a bit. If he liked it there, they would find an apartment together. Vance's mom started mailing them the classified section of a local newspaper and while on guard they would skim the apartment section. Vance would explain why the rent was cheaper in some places than others, and they would debate how close they needed to be to the beach.

I was a little nervous when I rang Vance's doorbell, but as soon as he opened that door and welcomed me in, it was just like the old times when I'd walk up to the third floor of the barracks and bang on his door to see if he wanted to hang out.

Reuniting with Old Friends

Vance was in high spirits. He had just gotten a job as a personal trainer at a local fitness club, which was all right for now. Even while in Mosul, Vance had a weight bench and dumbbells right outside his door where he would work out every day. One of the reasons he did a lot of heavy training over there was because he wanted to get back into competitive Muay Thai kickboxing, a passion of his, once he got back.

Callahan was surfing and living off the money he had saved in Iraq, as well as unemployment checks. California isn't exactly the cheapest place to live, and he mentioned something about having a difficult time trying to land an entry-level job, but he was confident all the same. He was sure that being a vet would somehow help him land a job, and he told me all about how he went down to the VA [Veterans Administration] and asked them if there were any entry-level jobs available for him that he could apply for, and the irritated lady behind the counter sternly told him, "We don't call them entry-level jobs here!" as she pointed at the bulletin board located right behind him displaying all available jobs. These were the kind of jobs that had "no college or experience necessary" listed under the qualifications. Most were file-clerk-type jobs, and he applied for all of them. One by one, he received letters in the mail briefly explaining that he was "not qualified."

At first he seemed like the same old Specialist Callahan that I knew back in the Army, but then he started showing me his surfboards and explaining to me in minute detail the social, spiritual, and technical differences between long boards and short boards, and I realized that maybe he had changed a little. I grew up in California, but nowhere near a surfable beach, and all this enthusiastic talk about swells, peaks, and tides was all completely foreign to me. Callahan now had a one-track mind, it was all about the beach and the waves, and being one with the ocean. "If I never had to worry about money or family or life, I would move to the ocean," Callahan told me. "I would live off the ocean, and some occasional Mexican food. I would spend every waking moment possible in the water, and I would be happy. Not the happy that Christmas morning brings, but a true and permanent happiness." I was stoked for him. He looked to be at peace, the most satisfied I had ever seen him. I was psyched that maybe the war hadn't changed him.

That night, we drank beers and exchanged war stories while watching one of Callahan's many surfing DVDs, *The Endless Summer*.

Finding a Job

The next day I drove back to L.A. glad that Vance and Callahan were doing well. We all kept in close touch through our MySpace profiles, e-mails, phone calls, and every now and then we'd drunk-dial each other and say a bunch of things that only we could say to each other. Things like "Nobody here knows, man" or "Nobody here cares."

Callahan finally found himself a job. He went down to a job-placement agency and told the lady working there that he was a returning veteran and in need of a job, any job, he didn't care, he just wanted to work. She asked him if he had a résumé, and he said no, not really, all he had done prior to that was fill out job applications. So she told him, "You're not going to leave this room today until you have a résumé saved on a disk," and she was going to help him write the thing. She asked him a bunch of questions, and when he looked at the final copy, he noticed that she downplayed all his combat experience. She explained that it would be easier for him to find a job that way. Specialist Callahan was a SAW [squad automatic weapons] gunner in my platoon, and once, in the middle of an ambush, under heavy enemy fire, he single-handedly put out a fire that was started when multiple RPGs [rocket-propelled grenades] hit his vehicle, taking out the engine in a huge fireball. There were nine men in that vehicle. I guess employers don't want to know that kind of stuff.

With a résumé now saved on disk, he sent it out to people who were looking to hire on Craigslist's help-wanted ads. He responded to three or four ads each day, finally landing a ten-dollar-an-hour packing job down at some shipping place packing fifty-pound boxes, putting labels on them, and moving them from one spot to another, five hundred boxes a day.

A couple months later, Callahan called me up to invite me to his going-away party.

"What do you mean a going-away party?" I said. "Are you *f--king crazy*? You can't move! Half the reason why I moved back to L.A. was because you and Vance live in San Diego! I thought you f--kin' loved it down there!"

"I do, man, but I can't find a real job. I've tried, but nobody will hire me, and I can't afford it here. I have family in Michigan. I can live with them."

"Ain't no waves in the Great Lakes, man!"

"There's waves out there."

"Not like the ones down here."

"I know, man, I know." . . .

Vets as Security Guards

Callahan had some medical marijuana that a friend of his scored at some cannabis club, and he asked what would be the best way to stash it in his car if he was driving cross-country. I told him that he didn't want to do that, and his best bet would be to smoke it up now so he wouldn't get busted having it on him in case he got pulled over, and of course I would help him out with that task. So we smoked it, and I passed out on his sofa. The next morning I woke up, said goodbye, and wished him luck.

The last time I talked to Callahan he was living in some part of greater Detroit, over by Nine Mile Road, and seemed pretty optimistic about prospects for a job as a security guard. I wonder how many security guards in the country are vets, because that would make four Operation Iraqi Freedom veterans that I know of who are now security guards. And that's not even including Cannon.

Nine times out of ten, if I get a phone call late at night, it's Cannon, who works the midnight-to-6:00-A.M. shift Monday through Friday as a nine-dollar-an-hour security guard in Seattle.

When he graduated from high school, Cannon got himself a full-time job in retail at the local shopping mall and enrolled full time at a nearby community college. His father, who worked for Boeing, helped him out with rent money so that he could concentrate on school, until his father was laid off. Cannon started working more and more hours at the mall and taking fewer classes. He started paying off his bills with his credit cards, going deeper into debt, at one point living off nothing but peanut butter straight from the jar. (Cannon claims that peanut butter provides enough nutrients for the human body to live on.) His grades dropped dramatically, pushing him to eventually drop out of school entirely. Thus, at age twenty, when he hit a point in his life where he was at less than zero, he joined the Army, kinda like I did at twenty-six.

Now he pulls the night shift guarding a parking lot. He makes sure that nobody breaks into any cars, and he proudly told me that only one car had been broken into during one of his shifts. He says you can usually tell by a person's body language whether they're up to no good. Also, car thieves like to wear hooded sweatshirts.

Cannon calls me up every two weeks or so to see how I'm doing and to find out if I'm ever going to be in the Seattle area again. "I might be heading up there soon," I told him one night. "Sergeant Horrocks sent me an invitation to his wedding in Montana."

"Horrocks is getting married? No way!"

Visiting an Old Roommate

I arrived at the Seattle/Tacoma airport and drove past Fort Lewis, down to Olympia. It seemed like every other car here in the King County and Puget Sound area had at least one or two yellow ribbons on it. Wow. Olympia is about a thirty-minute drive from Fort Lewis, and on Friday and Saturday nights we used to all pack into Sergeant Vance's Xterra (two in the front, three to four guys in the back, and sometimes one in the trunk) and go from bar to bar and try to drink Olympia dry.

I walked into that same bar we had gone to my last night, and the only thing I noticed that was different about it now was that the ashtrays were gone. After I drank a couple beers solo, Horrocks showed up. He looked exactly the same, a warm smile framed by a high and tight [military haircut]. We greeted each other, and the first thing I noticed about him was the mini combat-infantry lapel pin on his jacket collar, which of course he proudly pointed out to me. We sat at a table and ordered a couple drinks.

Horrocks and I had been roommates at Forward Operating Base Marez in Mosul for almost a year. We shared a room the size of a garage, and it was like Jack Lemmon and Walter Matthau [in the movie *The Odd Couple*], but somehow we became very good friends. We started catching up, and he told me all about how he had been sent over to RECON [reconnaissance] as an assistant team leader. RECON is where they send all the guys who are all "high speed" and "squared away." This didn't surprise me at all, as Horrocks was one of the best soldiers that I knew, and sincerely loves his occupation. He'll be going back to Iraq soon. I asked him how he felt about going back in RECON rather than in a regular infantry line squad, since RECON is a more dangerous job—sneak and peek in small teams. With a smile the old Horrocks that I knew back in Mosul came to life, and he said that he's more than happy to throw a few rounds downrange if need be, and the good news was that since I left they jacked up the maximum life insurance from $250,000 to more than $400,000. If they had done that before I got out, I just might have reenlisted.

Like me, Horrocks rarely ever goes out to bars. Maybe once in a blue moon he'll go out for a drink, but he always ends up leaving early, because it's just not the same anymore. . . .

"Born to Be Wild"

After a couple drinks, we got in the rental and headed to his apartment. I had promised Cannon that at midnight I would stop by his work and hang out with him, but there was one last bar that Horrocks insisted we go to together one last time.

He used to love going to this bar, so I made the detour. It was a workday, and when we got there, it was empty, the jukebox was silent and there was just an older AA [Alcoholics Anonymous]-looking couple nursing stiff drinks in the corner. We walked up to the bar and Horrocks ordered us Bud Lights and Jager [Jagermeister liqueur] shots, his trademark combination.

It finally hit me why Horrocks wanted to go to this bar so badly. It was the karaoke bar that he loved to get piss drunk and sing "Born to Be Wild" in. I've lost track of how many times I've seen him sing that song in this place. And Horrocks is the only person I know who can get a standing ovation every time; it was his song. He would be up onstage, mic in one hand, Bud Light in the other, singing his heart out. He didn't even have to look at the lyrics, he knew them all by heart. What was sad was that I didn't think I could ever picture him singing that song the same way again. Horrocks was no longer the hard-drinking wild man that I knew when I was in the Army. He was a lot more reserved.

While we were reminiscing, I caught myself paying particularly close attention to one of the empty tables over by the window.

The very last time I sat at that table was right before our deployment. I was with Specialist Blickenstaff, debating favorite metal bands over a couple beers. He was one of the first guys that I met when I arrived to the unit. His arms were covered in tattoos, and I recognized one of the tats he had—the logo of a band that I used to see play in small Bay Area clubs when I was younger. We'd always talk about music whenever we saw each other. It was at that table that I asked him if I could borrow some of his CDs so that I could burn them onto my iPod; the next day he loaned me a bunch. I forgot to return them before we deployed, and when we got to Kuwait, I apologized to him for that, and he told me not to worry about it, to just return them when we got back. I still have his CDs because Specialist Blickenstaff never made it back.

I suddenly felt guilty drinking in that bar after I realized that. No longer in the mood, we finished our beers and left. . . .

Attending a Wedding

I love weddings almost as much as I love stop-loss [compulsory extension of duty], PT tests [for physical fitness evaluation], parades, change-of-command ceremonies, beef-stew MREs ["meal, ready-to-eat"], the front-lean-and-rest position, and so on, so I usually try to avoid them altogether. I even avoided my own wedding by having it at a drive-through chapel in Vegas. But I was not going to avoid Horrocks's wedding.

I've been to In-N-Out Burgers bigger than the Butte airport. The flight to Montana was late due to weather conditions, so I called Horrocks to tell him that it might be a while before I got there. He was extremely cool about it, and he told me that he would be waiting at the airport with his soon-to-be-father-in-law, Jim, and he requested that I do him a huge favor and watch my language.

They were patiently waiting for me in the airport lobby. Jim had on jeans and real-life cowboy boots. He also had a cool mustache going on. I shook his hand, said hello, and we made our way to his Dodge Ram pickup truck. I looked around at the other parked vehicles and saw that all the other trucks in the parking lot were supersized as well.

Jim is a fish-and-game warden, and he talked quite a bit about his job—stories of poachers, bears, and drunk deer killers gone wild—which I found interesting.

When it came time to drop Jim off at home, Horrocks and I piled the eighty dollars' worth of beer he had bought for the wedding into the back of the new pickup truck he had bought immediately upon our return from Iraq so that he could go out in the woods and fish and hunt.

The cabins where we were to stay were located down a narrow dirt road that had nothing for miles and miles in either direction. I cracked open a beer as Horrocks informed me that Montana had recently passed an open-container law. We decided that if we got caught, we would just pretend that nobody told us about it. He then told me that when he and his wife went down to the courthouse to get their marriage license, the clerk made them both pledge out loud something about "as far as we know, we are not related."

The night was bright from the moon, and Montana looked like a safari park with nature gone wild in all directions, elk, deer, buffalo, and bunny rabbits running around freely all over the place. At one point a nice-sized buck bounded out about fifteen meters in front of our truck, crossed the road, and jumped over a tall fence. The only thing I'm used to having bound out in front of me in Los Angeles are coked-up celebrities fiddling with their goddamn iPods.

We passed a couple lonely cabins, and I was reminded of a finance brief we sat through right before we deployed to Iraq. We had a person explain to us all our benefits and the VA home loan to us, and at the end of the brief there was a Q&A [question-and-answer] session. I was sitting in one of the front rows, and somebody sitting in a row far behind me stood up and asked whether or not he could use his loan to buy some land out in the woods instead of a house, because he wanted to build a cabin on the land himself. I turned around in my seat, thinking to myself, Who the f--k is this Davy Crockett who wants to build a cabin in the woods? Do people even still live in cabins? I looked back and there was Horrocks.

The Wedding Ceremony

We arrived at the cabins with seventy dollars' worth of beer, and the next day I threw on some Banana Republic that my better half made me purchase a long time ago for an event that I had to look presentable for (and hadn't worn since) and walked over to the rough-hewn main cabin where the wedding was taking place. Horrocks was all dressed up in his Class-A uniform, with three full rows of ribbons and medals, blue cord and braided French fourragere, as well as a couple combat stripes on the sleeve. As much as I hated wearing the pickle-green Class-A uniform when I was in the Army, I kinda missed it now, standing there next to him in last season's argyle.

While waiting around for the wedding to start, the thirty or forty guests mingled, and eventually I got kinda peopled out, so I exited via the back door to sneak into the minus-20 weather for a smoke break. In the snow outside were several bottles of hard liquor that somebody had placed there to keep cold. As I was getting a smoke ready I overheard a couple people standing nearby laughing and talking about somebody singing "Born to Be Wild." I introduced myself as a friend of Horrocks's, and they told me about how the last time he was in Idaho, before he left for Iraq, they all took him out to the bars, and he karaoked "Born to Be Wild" and it was great, people loved him for it. I told them that I've seen him do the same thing in Washington—and loved him for it as well.

At the end of the wedding reception, Jim saw me standing around by myself and came up to me. We talked a little and he said, "I know you've heard this a lot already from many different people, but I just want to say that I'm glad that you made it back." I thanked him and told him that I was glad to be back as well. He went on to say that when he was in high school, there was this friend of his who graduated early because he was a really bright guy, and then he went off and joined the military, and a year later, in '66, he got killed in Vietnam. "I get sad whenever I think about that," Jim said, "because he had the best years of his life ahead of him, and he never got to experience them."

We stood there in silence and thought about that, and just then Sergeant Horrocks, looking like the happiest soldier, accompanied by his new wife, floated right by us, beaming to beat the band.

The war would wait. On this day, in distant Montana, the war didn't matter, nothing else in the whole world mattered.

Being the Wife of a Wounded Marine

Karie Fugett

In the following selection, Karie Fugett, the wife of a wounded marine, recalls seeing her husband for the first time after he was hurt. After learning of her husband's injuries, she travels with a friend to the National Naval Medical Center in Bethesda, Maryland. When she arrives, she visits her husband and is relieved to be reunited with him.

The day after Cleve's brother wrote me about Cleve being hurt, someone from the military called giving me more information about his injury and where he was at. They told me he had been flown to Germany and as soon as he was stable would leave there and head to Washington DC. I remember I had a pen and paper in my hand to keep notes so I would get every detail of what he said. Once I got off the phone I realized despite my efforts there was nothing but scribbles and sentences in no particular order. I was so tense with emotions. I was high from not sleeping, my head hurt from crying so much, I had run out of sane thoughts after thinking non stop since I heard the news, and I was just flat out scared of what I was going to find when I got to the hospital.

Shannon, being the amazing friend she is, offered to drive me up to DC. She wanted to be there for Cleve and I. Even if it were only for a few days. We just went ahead and packed as much of our stuff as we could into two suitcases, got all of her babies' stuff together, then sat and waited for the phone call. The next day the Liaison in DC called and said he had left Germany four hours prior and was on his way. I quickly

Karie Fugett, "Seeing Cleve for the First Time," *Being the Wife of a Wounded Marine*, July 17, 2008. Reproduced by permission of the author.

scribbled down the directions, we put our stuff in the car in a disturbing speed, and we took off.

That was a painful ride. I could hardly breathe and definitely could not relax. I think I was annoying Shannon a little with my constant rambling. She just kind of sat there in silence, driving as I asked "Are we almost there?", for the millionth time. That's just what I do when I'm nervous. I find someone, and I talk to them about whatever is on my mind. If you are around, you're it!

What kills me is, looking back (though I WAS scared) I had NO idea what was in store for me. My life was about to change more than I could've ever imagined.

Arriving at the Medical Center

Finally after driving through the night, we arrived at the National Naval Medical Center in Bethesda, MD. It was about midnight. I was sure no one would be there. Miraculously someone was. I remember thinking how hideous I looked. In my frenzy I forgot to brush my hair, put makeup on, or choose matching clothes. As quickly as I thought it, it went away. There were too many other things to think about.

The guy that met us gave me some paperwork to fill out. I swear the place we were sitting had the brightest lights I have ever seen. I felt like I was in a spotlight. They were hot too. I wasn't sure what the paperwork was for, but I figured if it's this late, he isn't going to make me do anymore than I have to because it's keeping him from being able to sleep too. I was too wired to concentrate long enough to read it anyway.

Seeing My Husband

I finally filled the paperwork out and we were off to see Cleve. I was so nervous. I didn't know what he would look like or what shape he would be in. I didn't know if he would be in pain. I didn't know what to say. I just knew I couldn't cry!!! I HAD to be strong for him! My chest was tight, and I remember just being so hot. I was tunnel visioning too. I saw nothing around me. I didn't care. I just wanted to get to Cleve.

Finally we got to his door. We had to put on these big yellow robes made of some kind of paper material and rubber gloves. Needless to say it wasn't helping my being hot very much. We went into the room and there he was. I thought he was asleep at first but the guy we were with tapped on the door and Cleve's head popped up. He was so drugged up. "Heeeeeeey. . . .", he said. "Hi baby". I didn't know what else to say! He actually seemed pretty happy! Whatever they had him on was the good stuff for sure. I just walked up to him really slowly. It was kind of dark in there. The only light on was one across the room. His leg was covered but his arm was out. His hand had been hit by some shrapnel so it had to be bandaged and somehow this gigantic piece of foam in the shape of swiss cheese was helping it heal. That was one of the first things I noticed (How odd . . .). I got right up next to him, teared up and just looked at him. I was afraid to touch him because I didn't know where all he hurt. He lifted his fingers motioning me to hold his hand. I did. I just asked if he was ok. He said he was. I gave him a kiss as lightly as I could so I wouldn't hurt anything.

Shannon had been waiting in the waiting room because babies aren't allowed near the guys. She just let me have my time with him and waited until the next day to see him herself. I didn't stay long because it was late and everyone needed to rest. I knew he was in good hands and I knew (Because now I had seen him!) that he was ok.

My Journey with an Iraqi Refugee

Jennifer Utz

Videojournalist Jennifer Utz tells the story in the following article of how she helped an Iraqi man immigrate to the United States. Like many Iraqis, her friend Mohamed fled Iraq because of the war and was forced to live in the slums of Syria. She explains that Mohamed worked as a model, but after the invasion of Iraq, he was forced to leave, partially because of his sexual orientation. Utz helped Mohamed begin the process of seeking asylum in the United States, and after a year and a half of effort, he was allowed to immigrate. While Utz and Mohamed were happy at their success, they realize that many other refugees remain in Syria and Jordan.

"That one sounds like mortar fire," Mohamed said to me. "And that was definitely a sniper." My Iraqi friend and I were in Coney Island [New York] for the Friday night summer fireworks. Listening to the thunderous explosions over the water as we rode the Wonder Wheel, memories of life in war-torn Iraq inevitably came to mind.

I wondered what else must be going through his head. Just two weeks ago, he had been a refugee living in the slums of Damascus, Syria.

To date, 1 in 5 Iraqis have left their homes. Two million have left the country, and another two and a half million are internally displaced. After the 2003 bombing of the Shiite shrine in Samarra unleashed a wave of sectarian clashes, those with the means to do so began fleeing in droves. Many have chosen to wait out the violence in urban areas of Jordan and Syria, the two countries that host the most Iraqi refugees.

Jennifer Utz, "From Baghdad to Brooklyn: My Journey with an Iraqi Refugee," *Huffington Post*, November 19, 2008. Reproduced by permission of the author.

Mohamed had been living like most of them. Unable to work legally in Syria, he relied on the meager savings his parents could send him from Iraq. Over the course of one year, he moved 16 times to a series of filthy, roach-infested, overpriced apartments. It's a seller's market. Iraqi refugees are taken advantage of by just about every crooked landlord who realizes how desperately they don't want to be sent back—war profiteering on a new level.

Meeting Mohamed

I first met Mohamed in 2007, when I interviewed him for a video piece on refugees. We became fast friends and during my time working in Syria, we spent our days exploring Damascus, a city foreign to both of us.

There during the presidential referendum, we found that Mohamed's Western appearance made for some interesting fun. We crashed referendum parties and told the revelers that we were both models from New York City—everyone from average citizens to high government officials wanted a photo with "the foreigners." Little did they know, Mohamed was one of the 1.2 million Iraqi refugees who were placing a severe economic, social and political burden on their country.

The more I got to know him, the more I wanted to document his life. Yet at the same time, sitting by and simply watching his life unravel didn't seem right to me.

I wanted to bring Mohamed to the United States. The eternal optimist, I took a photo of a bench on the Brooklyn Heights Promenade, where one can take in the quintessential view of Manhattan. "We'll be sitting there together one day," I promised him.

I spent a collective five months in Damascus with Mohamed. Throughout this journey—at times both tragic and entertaining—I made a good friend, became part of an Iraqi family and realized the reach of the power that I have as a U.S. citizen in doing my part to clean up the mess that's been made in Iraq.

Life Before the Invasion

The son of a diplomat and an attorney, Mohamed's middle-class family lived in a large house in central Baghdad.

Socially, his life was not unlike that of men his same age living in a Western culture. As a teenager, he joined a garage rock band. His father begged him to cut his long hair, disapproved of his attire and was incensed when he got a tattoo.

Obsessed with American culture, he taught himself English by watching American sitcoms and music videos, covering the Arabic subtitles on his television with black tape. His two favorite shows were *Friends* and *Frasier*.

Unfortunately, what passed for teenage antics was not condoned as he came of age, and his American affectations became the subject of suspicion and ridicule. He also had romantic feelings toward men, but coming out was not an option.

Despite being a cultural outsider, life was manageable. Scouted by a modeling agency at the age of 18, a new world opened up to him. He flew to Lebanon and Turkey and had his first taste of life outside a culture he [found] too restrictive for someone like him. Sipping champagne at fashion industry parties and kissing a man for the first time, he felt truly alive.

Mohamed's budding modeling career came to an abrupt halt in March of 2003, when, in the middle of his 20th birthday party, his country was invaded and the war began.

In 2005, a note arrived on his family's front doorstep: "Get your gay son out of the country or we'll kill the whole family." Two weeks later, Mohamed's tearful mother put him on a plane to Jordan.

Seeking Asylum, Pleading for His Life

When a refugee arrives in a host country, they have the option to register with UNHCR [United Nations refugee agency] after which they submit to a series of interviews with the agency.

UNHCR primarily keeps track of and distributes aid to refugee populations. In rare cases, UNHCR refers them for resettlement to another country. This would be our ultimate goal for Mohamed.

I encouraged him to open up about his homosexuality, since it was pertinent to his case. In the fall of 2005, Grand Ayatollah Ali al-Sistani called for the killing of homosexuals "in the worst, most severe way possible." As a result, a spate of brutal attacks against homosexuals began throughout the country.

Being "different" was something Mohamed had considered a curse his whole life. Now we hoped it could turn into a blessing.

I sent Mohamed's story to a number of people in positions of power. Representatives from Human Rights Watch and Refugees International, and openly gay [Wisconsin] Congresswoman Tammy Baldwin, gave me letters of support on his behalf.

Using connections I'd made as a journalist, I presented Mohamed's case to a representative at UNHCR. She sent his full dossier to the Senior Protection Officer. The next day, he received a call—instead of having to wait six months for an interview, like most Iraqis, he would be seen right away.

The night before his interview, Mohamed crouched before my feet on the floor of my apartment, desperately sorting through the pile of documents he'd had to scramble together before his swift departure from Iraq. His passport, personal IDs, modeling contracts and college graduation certificates were the only proof of his former life.

Here he was—preparing to meet with a complete stranger working for an enormous bureaucratic organization, to plead for his life.

Mohamed went through four UNHCR interviews, and ultimately, was recommended for resettlement to the United States. It was a huge reason to celebrate, but certainly not the end of the road.

He would spend the next eight months anxiously waiting to meet with representatives from the United States.

These multiple "life interviews" were humiliating and exhausting. Mohamed interviewed four times with the State Department, each time recounting the painful story of his two years in exile. Before meeting with The Department of Homeland Security, he realized that this moment would shape the rest of his life.

This time, the questions were tougher. "Have you ever had sex with a man?" Mohamed found this too personal to answer. He was also forced to sign the Selective Service Registration forms, stating that if there was a draft, he may have to go back and serve in Iraq. This further unnerved him.

Over the next few months, Mohamed's heart raced every time the phone rang, as he hoped it was news he wanted to hear.

Mohamed's Family

Soon Christmas arrived, and Mohamed's mother and extended family came to spend the holidays with him. Having been apart from his young nieces for close to a year, Mohamed was saddened that they'd developed the same habits of the adults in the house—staying up throughout the night and sleeping all day. The lifestyle had taken its toll. Five-year-old Noona's skin had become jaundiced from lack of sun.

Unaware of the severity of the situation, she kept asking her parents to take her back to Baghdad so she could play with her friends. As a Westerner, I tried to provide her with new distractions. We played hide-and-seek, had fun with coloring books, and became so close that she insisted on sleeping with me every night.

Mohamed's mother, once an established civil rights lawyer, was hoping to return to work in Baghdad. She had asked me to bring her a large bag that looked like a purse—something big enough to carry her files, but inconspicuous enough to not draw attention to her as a lawyer, since professionals have been targets for murder in Iraq.

She shared with me her feelings of degradation and loss, both of her career and her now struggling family. "I used to work. I wasn't only sitting around the home, preparing meals and watching television, like you see me now. We used to have a good life in Baghdad."

Through this family, I met a broken people, Iraqis living in a physical and emotional void, yet trying desperately to hold on to some vestiges of their former selves.

Good News, and a New Life

In July 2008, I got the call we'd been waiting for. After one and a half years of advocacy, Mohamed had been accepted as a refugee.

He flew to New York a month later, and I started introducing him to life in the United States. I taught him how to navigate the subway system, gave him advice on finding a job, and struggled to explain our confusing health care system. The U.S. government would provide Mohamed with Medicaid, food stamps, and a stipend of $240 per month, as well as $900 toward rent. But the financial benefits only last for three months; he had to get acclimated quickly.

Mohamed is staying with me in Brooklyn as he gets on his feet. I see him going through various stages of excitement, optimism and fear on a daily basis. After having lived in forced stagnation for over four years, it's hard to find the motivation and confidence to revisit the dreams he once had.

The Exception, Not the Rule

In recent months, much has been said in the media about Iraqi refugees going back to Iraq as a result of the success of "the surge" [a large influx of American troops]. The truth is that most of those who return are doing so because either they've run out of money or their visas have expired. Many of those who return find that another family has taken up residence in their home.

After receiving criticism for not having done enough to respond to the crisis, the [George W.] Bush administration recently began taking in more Iraqi refugees—in 2008, more than 14,000 Iraqis were accepted into the United States. But for the country that started this war, that's a drop in the bucket—just a third of 1 percent of the total number of those displaced. After the Vietnam War, hundreds of thousands of Southeast Asians were authorized and ensured admission to the United States each year.

Today, Mohamed says that without having had me as an advocate, he could have never done this on his own. As an American and a journalist, I was able to make him stand out as more than a face in the crowd, and helped him navigate the perplexing bureaucracy of being a refugee.

His painful story is one of many. Mohamed and I sit on "our bench" frequently, taking in the magnificent view of Manhattan and reveling in our victory, but we can't help but remember all those who were left behind.

CHAPTER 3

The Debate on the Iraq War

Avoiding an Unnecessary War

Jim McDermott

In the following selection, Jim McDermott delivers a floor speech to the U.S. House of Representatives in late 2002 arguing that diplomacy can still prevent war with Iraq. He lists four reasons why the war should be opposed. First, he states, progress is being made with disarming Iraq through the redeployment of United Nations weapon inspectors. Secondly, he notes that since there is little support for military action, a war with Iraq would strain international relations. Thirdly, McDermott points to the potential human cost of both American military personnel and Iraqi civilians. Finally, he opposes a war with Iraq because it is not a war of self-defense, but a war of empire.

We are standing at the abyss of a horrifying war. President [George W.] Bush himself told us Monday night [October 7, 2002,] that this war was neither "imminent nor unavoidable." And yet we are pushing, hurrying, racing against time to give the President our approval of a future war, a war without limits or boundaries, a war waged because the President thinks diplomacy has failed.

I do not believe diplomacy has failed. And I do not believe we have to go to war. President Bush's speech was designed to frighten the American people, and to intimidate the United Nations. It wasn't address[ed] to us, the Congress, because President Bush and his advisers already believe that they have our backing. But they don't have the backing of the American people. The polls tell us that. Our constituents tell us that. The phone calls and faxes and emails and letters to our offices, running 100 to one, 500 to one against this war, all tell us that. I, for one, am not afraid. And I do not think my col-

Representative Jim McDermott, "Authorization for Use of Military Force Against Iraq Resolution of 2002," *Congressional Record*, vol. 148, no. 133, October 10, 2002.

leagues in the House and in the Senate should be afraid either. We should not be afraid of standing up to an unnecessary war. We should not be afraid to stand up to a President when he is wrong. We should not be afraid of the American people; they are right.

President Bush tells us how important it is, for his campaign to win support in the United Nations, that we here in the United States speak with one voice. But we do not have only one voice; we cannot and will not lend our voices to support a war that we know is wrong. When my colleagues and I went to Iraq, we went to tell the Iraqis that they must allow free and unfettered U.N. inspections. We went to investigate the situation facing Iraqi civilians after 12 years of crippling economic sanctions. And we went knowing that our democracy is strengthened when we see, and hear, and learn and debate all sides. We didn't have to go to Iraq to know why we're against going to war against Iraq. There are plenty of reasons back home to oppose this juggernaut towards a unilateral preemptive strike on Iraq.

Let U.N. Inspectors Do Their Job

The first reason is that disarmament should be on top of our Iraq agenda. And getting the United Nations inspectors back in should be the first step towards accomplishing that task. The U.N. must be allowed to take the lead; their inspectors were already close to finishing work on the technical arrangements so they could get to work right away. Iraq had proposed the inspection team arrive as early as October 16th.

Initial meetings between Iraqi and U.N. officials were held in March of this year to begin discussions about the return of inspectors to Iraq after they had been excluded for almost four years. Further meetings were held in May and again on the 4th of July. That July meeting was particularly useful, coming in the context of growing international pressure on Iraq and seeming to set the stage for the serious possibility of inspectors returning to Baghdad. But the next day, July 5th, the Pentagon leaked its latest provocative war plan to the *New York Times*, calling for a major air attack and land invasion to "topple Saddam Hussein." The Iraqis pulled back.

But pressure continued to build, and in August the Iraqi Parliament invited members of Congress to come to Baghdad with inspectors of our choosing and to look for ourselves. On September 13th I went to New York to meet with Iraqi Foreign Minister Naji Sabri, and told him I would accept his invitation to Iraq with the understanding that the inspectors I would choose to accompany me would be the UNMOVIC [United Nations Monitoring, Verification and Inspection Commission] inspectors themselves. We talked about the absolute necessity of the U.N. resuming unfettered inspections in Iraq, and he said they were ready for such inspections, and they understood that if no weapons were found the Security Council would lift the economic sanctions. I made no promises except to say I would come. Forty-eight hours later, on September 16, Sabri told [U.N. Secretary General] Kofi Annan that Iraq was prepared to accept the inspectors back into Iraq.

Unfortunately, instead of welcoming this development, it became clear that the Bush administration was not prepared to take Iraq's "yes" for an answer. The State Department's answer to the long-delayed Iraqi acquiescence was to announce that it was now in "thwart mode," determined to prevent the inspections from going forward. . . .

A Negative Impact

The second reason we should oppose this war has to do with its impact on our relations with allies all over the world. There is virtually no international support, at the governmental or public level, for a U.S. attack on Iraq. Our closest allies throughout Europe, in Canada, and elsewhere, have made clear their opposition to a military invasion. While they recognize the Iraqi regime as a brutal, undemocratic regime, they do not support a unilateral preemptive military assault as an appropriate response to that regime. Our European friends are pleading with us not to go to war, reminding us that disarmament, starting with inspections, is their goal. Russia and China say the same thing. Are we to simply ignore our friends' opinions and go it alone?

Throughout the Middle East, the Arab states, including our closest allies, have made unequivocal their opposition to an invasion of Iraq. Even Kuwait, once the target of Iraqi military occupation and ostensibly the most vulnerable to Iraqi threats, has moved to normalize its relations with Baghdad. The Arab League–sponsored rapprochement [accord] between Iraq and Kuwait at the March 2002 Arab Summit is now underway, including such long-overdue moves as the return of Kuwait's national archives. Iraq has now repaired its relation with every Arab country, and not a single one of Iraq's neighbors publicly supports a U.S. war. Turkey has refused to publicly announce its agreement to allow use of its air bases, and Jordan and other Arab countries have made clear their urgent plea for the U.S. to abjure a military attack on Iraq.

Again, it is certainly unlikely that a single government in the region would ultimately stand against a U.S. demand for base rights, use of airspace or overflight rights, or access to any other facilities. The question we must answer therefore is not whether our allies will ultimately accede to our wishes, but just how high a price are we prepared to exact from our allies? Virtually every Arab government, especially those most closely tied to the U.S. (Jordan and Egypt, perhaps even Saudi Arabia) will face dramatically escalated popular opposition. The existing crisis of legitimacy faced by these non-representative regimes, absolute monarchies and president-for-life style democratics, will be seriously exacerbated by a U.S. invasion of Iraq. Region-wide instability may be expected to result, and some of those governments might even face the possibility of being overthrown.

In the entire Middle East region, only Israel supports the U.S. build-up to war in Iraq. Prime Minister [Ariel] Sharon has made no secret of his view that the chaos caused by a U.S. attack on Iraq might well provide him with the opportunity for a large-scale escalation against the Palestinians.

When President Bush repeats his mantra that "you are either with us or with the terrorists," no government in the world wants to stand defiant. But a foreign policy based on international coercion and our allies' fear of retaliation for noncompliance, is not a policy that will protect Americans and our place in the world.

The Human Toll of War

Still another reason to oppose this has to do with the human toll. During the Vietnam war, I was lieutenant commander in the U.S. Navy Medical Corps. My job, as a psychiatrist, was to treat young soldiers who returned from that war terribly damaged by what they saw and what they suffered. I carry those memories with me still.

While official estimates of casualties among U.S. service personnel are not public, we can be certain they will be much higher than in the current war in Afghanistan. We do know, from Pentagon estimates of two years ago, the likely death toll among Iraqi civilians: about 10,000 Iraqi civilians would be killed.

The most recent leaked military plan for invading Iraq, the so-called "inside-out" plan based on a relatively small contingent of U.S. ground troops with heavy reliance on air strikes, would focus first and primarily on Baghdad. In fact, all of the leaked military plans begin with air assaults on Baghdad. The Iraqi capital is described as being ringed with Saddam Hussein's crack troops and studded with anti-aircraft batteries. Those charges may or may not be true. But what is never mentioned in the military planning documents is the inconvenient fact that Baghdad is also a crowded city of five million or more people; a heavy air bombardment would cause the equivalent human catastrophe of—and look very similar to—a heavy air bombardment of Los Angeles. . . .

I traveled with my colleagues to the southern [Iraqi] city of Basra, where we heard from physicians that the first question new mothers ask after giving birth is not whether the baby is a boy or a girl, but whether it is normal or not— because the rates of birth defects are so high. Many think those high rates of birth defects, skyrocketing rates of leukemia and other cancers, have something to do with the depleted uranium [DU] weapons our military used so efficiently during the [first Gulf] war 12 years ago.

Many of our own Gulf War veterans—and their children— are also suffering higher than normal rates of cancers and birth defects. And the Veterans Administration medical care budget has just been slashed. Do we want to go to war again, a war that will cost perhaps $60 to $100 billion, and create a whole new generation of wounded veterans, along with too many who will not come home at all? We have not yet heard an answer from the Pentagon to the question of how they plan to protect our men and women in uniform—as well as vulnerable Iraqi civilians—from the danger of depleted uranium weapons. So far the Pentagon has still not conducted the full-scale scientific study of the impact of DU on the human body. We should not go to war to use our troops as guinea pigs again.

A War of Empire

I oppose this war because it is a war of empire, not of legitimate self-defense. We claim to be a nation of laws. But too often we are prepared to put aside the requirements of international law and the United Nations Charter to which we hold other nations appropriately accountable. . . .

President Bush's October 7th speech was clearly designed to frighten the American people. Once again that speech dis-

Iraqi government, would be the replacement of the current re-gime with one virtually indistinguishable from it except for the man at the top. In February 2002 *Newsweek* magazine profiled the five leaders said to be on Washington's short list of candidates to replace Saddam Hussein. The Administration has not publicly issued such a list of its own, but it certainly typifies the model the U.S. has in mind. All five of the candi-dates were high-ranking officials within the Iraqi military un-til the mid-1990s. All five have been linked to the use of chemical weapons by the military; at least one admits it. The legitimacy of going to war against a country to replace a bru-tal military leader with another brutal leader must be chal-lenged.

A Bloody Occupation

And whoever is installed in Baghdad by victorious U.S. troops, it is certain that a long and possibly bloody occupation would follow. The price would be high; Iraqis know better than we do how their government has systematically denied them civil and political rights. But they hold us responsible for stripping them of their economic and social rights—the right to suffi-cient food, clear water, education, medical care—that together form the other side of the human rights equation. Economic sanctions have devastated Iraqi society. After twelve years those in Washington who believe that Iraqis accept the popu-lar inside-the-Beltway [within D.C.] mantra that "sanctions aren't responsible, Saddam Hussein is responsible" for hunger and deprivation in Iraq, are engaged in wishful thinking. The notion that everyone in Iraq will welcome as "liberators" those whom most Iraqis hold responsible for 12 years of crippling sanctions is simply naive. Basing military strategy on such wishful speculation becomes very dangerous—in particular for U.S. troops themselves.

A U.S. invasion of Iraq would risk the lives of U.S. mili-tary personnel and kill potentially thousands of Iraqi civilians;

it is not surprising that many U.S. military officers, including some within the Joint Chiefs of Staff, are publicly opposed to a new war against Iraq. Such an attack would violate international law and the U.N. Charter, and isolate us from our friends and allies around the world. An invasion would complicate the return of U.N. arms inspectors, and will cost billions of dollars urgently needed at home. And at the end of the day, an invasion will not insure stability, let alone democracy, in Iraq or the rest of the volatile Middle east region. Rather, it will put American civilians at greater risk than they are today.

We need disarmament, not a war for empire, oil, or "regime change." We need the U.N. inspectors to go in and finish their work. Until they do, we simply don't know what weapons Iraq has or doesn't have.

Let us not go to war, in pursuit of oil or the blandishments of empire. War is too important and its consequences too disastrous.

The Reasons for War

George W. Bush

In the following selection, U.S. president George W. Bush, in a March 18, 2003 speech, delivers an ultimatum to Iraq: disarm or face military consequences. Iraq, the president explains, has a history of aggression, and both the United Nations and Congress have approved of the use of military force to eradicate Iraq's weapons program. Any military action by the United States against Iraq, however, is not an action against the Iraqi people, Bush states. In anticipation of military action in Iraq, Bush notes, security measures have also been heightened in the United States. All of these actions, he believes, will keep Americans safe and offer the Iraqi people a chance for freedom.

My fellow citizens, events in Iraq have now reached the final days of decision. For more than a decade, the United States and other nations have pursued patient and honorable efforts to disarm the Iraqi regime without war. That regime pledged to reveal and destroy all its weapons of mass destruction as a condition for ending the Persian Gulf War in 1991.

Since then, the world has engaged in 12 years of diplomacy. We have passed more than a dozen resolutions in the United Nations Security Council. We have sent hundreds of weapons inspectors to oversee the disarmament of Iraq. Our good faith has not been returned.

The Iraqi regime has used diplomacy as a ploy to gain time and advantage. It has uniformly defied Security Council resolutions demanding full disarmament. Over the years, U.N. weapon inspectors have been threatened by Iraqi officials, electronically bugged, and systematically deceived. Peaceful efforts to disarm the Iraqi regime have failed again and again—

George W. Bush, "Ultimatum Speech," C-Span, March 18, 2003. http://www.c-span.org/executive/bush_saddam.asp?Cat=Current_Event&Code=Bush_Admin.

because we are not dealing with peaceful men. Intelligence gathered by this and other governments leaves no doubt that the Iraq regime continues to possess and conceal some of the most lethal weapons ever devised. This regime has already used weapons of mass destruction against Iraq's neighbors and against Iraq's people.

A History of Reckless Aggression

The regime has a history of reckless aggression in the Middle East. It has a deep hatred of America and our friends. And it has aided, trained and harbored terrorists, including operatives of al Qaeda. The danger is clear: using chemical, biological or, one day, nuclear weapons, obtained with the help of Iraq, the terrorists could fulfill their stated ambitions and kill thousands or hundreds of thousands of innocent people in our country, or any other.

The United States and other nations did nothing to deserve or invite this threat. But we will do everything to defeat it. Instead of drifting along toward tragedy, we will set a course toward safety. Before the day of horror can come, before it is too late to act, this danger will be removed.

The United States of America has the sovereign authority to use force in assuring its own national security. That duty falls to me, as Commander-in-Chief, by the oath I have sworn, by the oath I will keep.

U.N. and Congressional Support

Recognizing the threat to our country, the United States Congress voted overwhelmingly last year to support the use of force against Iraq. America tried to work with the United Nations to address this threat because we wanted to resolve the issue peacefully. We believe in the mission of the United Nations. One reason the U.N. was founded after the second world war was to confront aggressive dictators, actively and early, before they can attack the innocent and destroy the peace.

In the case of Iraq, the Security Council did act, in the early 1990s. Under Resolutions 678 and 687—both still in effect—the United States and our allies are authorized to use force in ridding Iraq of weapons of mass destruction. This is not a question of authority, it is a question of will.

Last September [2002], I went to the U.N. General Assembly and urged the nations of the world to unite and bring an end to this danger. On November 8th, the Security Council unanimously passed Resolution 1441, finding Iraq in material breach of its obligations, and vowing serious consequences if Iraq did not fully and immediately disarm.

American Resolve

Today, no nation can possibly claim that Iraq has disarmed. And it will not disarm so long as Saddam Hussein holds power. For the last four-and-a-half months, the United States and our allies have worked within the Security Council to enforce that Council's long-standing demands. Yet, some permanent members of the Security Council have publicly announced they will veto any resolution that compels the disarmament of Iraq. These governments share our assessment of the danger, but not our resolve to meet it. Many nations, however, do have the resolve and fortitude to act against this threat to peace, and a broad coalition is now gathering to enforce the just demands of the world. The United Nations Security Council has not lived up to its responsibilities, so we will rise to ours.

In recent days, some governments in the Middle East have been doing their part. They have delivered public and private messages urging the dictator to leave Iraq, so that disarmament can proceed peacefully. He has thus far refused. All the decades of deceit and cruelty have now reached an end. Saddam Hussein and his sons must leave Iraq within 48 hours. Their refusal to do so will result in military conflict, commenced at a time of our choosing. For their own safety, all foreign nationals—including journalists and inspectors—should leave Iraq immediately.

Message to Iraq

Many Iraqis can hear me tonight in a translated radio broadcast, and I have a message for them. If we must begin a military campaign, it will be directed against the lawless men who rule your country and not against you. As our coalition takes away their power, we will deliver the food and medicine you need. We will tear down the apparatus of terror and we will help you to build a new Iraq that is prosperous and free. In a free Iraq, there will be no more wars of aggression against your neighbors, no more poison factories, no more executions of dissidents, no more torture chambers and rape rooms. The tyrant will soon be gone. The day of your liberation is near.

It is too late for Saddam Hussein to remain in power. It is not too late for the Iraqi military to act with honor and protect your country by permitting the peaceful entry of coalition forces to eliminate weapons of mass destruction. Our forces will give Iraqi military units clear instructions on actions they can take to avoid being attacked and destroyed. I urge every member of the Iraqi military and intelligence services, if war comes, do not fight for a dying regime that is not worth your own life.

And all Iraqi military and civilian personnel should listen carefully to this warning. In any conflict, your fate will depend on your action. Do not destroy oil wells, a source of wealth that belongs to the Iraqi people. Do not obey any command to use weapons of mass destruction against anyone, including the Iraqi people. War crimes will be prosecuted. War criminals will be punished. And it will be no defense to say, "I was just following orders."

Should Saddam Hussein choose confrontation, the American people can know that every measure has been taken to avoid war, and every measure will be taken to win it. Americans understand the costs of conflict because we have paid them in the past. War has no certainty, except the certainty of sacrifice. Yet, the only way to reduce the harm and duration of war is to apply the full force and might of our military, and we are prepared to do so. If Saddam Hussein attempts to cling to power, he will remain a deadly foe until the end. In desperation, he and terrorists groups might try to conduct terrorist operations against the American people and our friends. These attacks are not inevitable. They are, however, possible. And this very fact underscores the reason we cannot live under the threat of blackmail. The terrorist threat to America and the world will be diminished the moment that Saddam Hussein is disarmed.

Fighting Terrorism

Our government is on heightened watch against these dangers. Just as we are preparing to ensure victory in Iraq, we are taking further actions to protect our homeland. In recent days, American authorities have expelled from the country certain individuals with ties to Iraqi intelligence services. Among other measures, I have directed additional security of our airports, and increased Coast Guard patrols of major seaports. The Department of Homeland Security is working closely with the nation's governors to increase armed security at critical facilities across America.

Should enemies strike our country, they would be attempting to shift our attention with panic and weaken our morale with fear. In this, they would fail. No act of theirs can alter the course or shake the resolve of this country. We are a peaceful people—yet we're not a fragile people, and we will not be intimidated by thugs and killers. If our enemies dare to strike us, they and all who have aided them, will face fearful consequences.

We are now acting because the risks of inaction would be far greater. In one year, or five years, the power of Iraq to inflict harm on all free nations would be multiplied many times over. With these capabilities, Saddam Hussein and his terrorist allies could choose the moment of deadly conflict when they are strongest. We choose to meet that threat now, where it arises, before it can appear suddenly in our skies and cities.

The cause of peace requires all free nations to recognize new and undeniable realities. In the 20th century, some chose to appease murderous dictators, whose threats were allowed to grow into genocide and global war. In this century, when evil men plot chemical, biological and nuclear terror, a policy of appeasement could bring destruction of a kind never before seen on this earth.

Terrorists and terror states do not reveal these threats with fair notice, in formal declarations—and responding to such enemies only after they have struck first is not self-defense, it is suicide. The security of the world requires disarming Saddam Hussein now.

Honoring Liberty

As we enforce the just demands of the world, we will also honor the deepest commitments of our country. Unlike Saddam Hussein, we believe the Iraqi people are deserving and capable of human liberty. And when the dictator has departed, they can set an example to all the Middle East of a vital and peaceful and self-governing nation.

The United States, with other countries, will work to advance liberty and peace in that region. Our goal will not be achieved overnight, but it can come over time. The power and appeal of human liberty is felt in every life and every land. And the greatest power of freedom is to overcome hatred and violence, and turn the creative gifts of men and women to the pursuits of peace.

That is the future we choose. Free nations have a duty to defend our people by uniting against the violent. And tonight, as we have done before, America and our allies accept that responsibility. Good night, and may God continue to bless America.

The Madness of War Profiteering

Robert Greenwald

In the following selection, documentary filmmaker Robert Green-
wald testifies to Congress on war profiteering in Iraq. In a num-
ber of instances, Greenwald notes, military contractors are fre-
quently trained by army personnel but are paid three times more
for the same job. He also points to a number of instances where
contractors have billed the government for extravagant expenses
and submitted inflated invoices. As a result, contractors are
wasting billions of taxpayer dollars and putting the lives of
workers at risk.

I appreciate the opportunity to share with you what I have
learned in the course of making the documentary film, *Iraq
For Sale: The War Profiteers.* Along with my colleagues at Brave
New Films, I spent a year researching the experiences of soldiers, truck drivers and families affected by the presence of
private military contractors in Iraq. They shared with us their
harrowing experiences of how military privatization and war
profiteering have affected their lives, and in some cases taken
the life of a loved one.

It is their personal stories that compel me to testify today.
I am not a lawyer or a financial specialist or a government ex-
pert, but I can tell you from my extensive first-hand experience with these folks that something is seriously wrong. We
are hurting our country and the many patriots who serve in
the military. Our taxpayer dollars are being spent, abused,
mis-used, and wasted on profiteers. It is a true tragedy, and it
is costing the lives of Americans and Iraqis.

Please let me introduce you to a few of these people and
their stories.

Robert Greenwald, "The Madness of the War Profiteering in Iraq," *AlterNet*, May 10,
2007. Reproduced by permission of the author.

Iraq for Sale

Imagine someone with the exact same job as you, working next to you, but getting paid three times as much as you! We heard this story over and over again from the soldiers we interviewed. And in the case of US Army SPC David Mann, a radio repair technician who served in Iraq, he was even required to train KBR [a subsidiary of oilfield services giant Halliburton] contractors to replace him. In *Iraq For Sale*, David shared his frustration:

"When I could be actively becoming a better soldier and becoming more proficient in my job, instead I'm going to sit up on guard duty and wait around while KBR contractors are doing the job that I had to train them to do."

US Army specialist Anthony Lagouranis also spoke of the effects of the private contractors on the military:

"It certainly affected retention because I don't know why any military person would re-enlist to do the same job when they could get out of the military and make six times the money—I really don't understand why they were outsourced. I mean, it seems like this is a military job and the military should be doing it. Especially because the more civilians you have out there, the more military people you need to guard them. So we're spreading us thin."

Iraq For Sale was seen by hundreds of thousands of people around the country, and I cannot tell you the number of soldiers who saw it and thanked us for exposing the toll that contracting and profiteering are taking on our armed forces and on the war in Iraq.

Waste in Iraq

I was also appalled to learn of the amount of waste by contractors in Iraq.

I remember clearly my interview with Stewart Scott, a former Halliburton employee. With pain and rage in his voice, he said how dare Halliburton put its people up at five-star hotels, while the soldiers, who he was there to help, were sleeping on the ground. I did not believe him at first, but then he began naming the hotels and the locations. It was all true.

I also spoke with Shane Ratliff, a truck driver from Ruby, South Carolina.

He saw Halliburton advertising a job for truck drivers in Iraq and he signed up. When Shane started telling me that empty trucks were being driven across dangerous stretches of desert, I assumed he was mistaken. Why would they do that? Then he explained that Halliburton got paid for the number of trips they took, regardless of whether they were carrying anything. These unnecessary trips where putting the lives of truckers at risk, exposing drivers and co-workers to attack. This was the result of cost-plus, no-bid contracts.

Another young Halliburton worker named James Logsdon told me about the burn pits. Burn pits are large dumps near military stations where they would burn equipment, trucks, trash, etc. If they ordered the wrong item, they'd throw it in the burn pit. If a tire blew on a piece of equipment, they'd throw the whole thing into the burn pit. The burn pits had so much equipment, they even gave them a nickname—"Home Depot."

The trucker said he would get us some photos. And I naively asked, how big are they, the size of a backyard swimming pool? He laughed, and referred to one that he had seen that was 15 football fields large, and burned around the clock! It infuriated him to have to burn stuff rather then give it to the Iraqis or to the military. Yet Halliburton was being rewarded each time they billed the government for a new truck or new piece of equipment. With a cost-plus contract, the contractors receive a percentage of the money they spend. As Shane told me, "It's a legal way of stealing from the government or the taxpayers' money."

These costs eat up the money that could be used for other supplies.

Sgt. Phillip Slocum wrote to us and said, "In previous experiences I went off to war with extra everything, and then some. This time however, Uncle Sam sent me off with one pair of desert boots, two uniforms, and body armor that didn't fit."

Contractor Misbehavior

Cost-plus and no-bid contracts are hopelessly undermining our efforts and costing the taxpayers billions. They do not operate within a free-market system and have no competition, but instead create a Stalinist system of rewarding cronies [as occurred in the early Soviet Union under its leader Joseph Stalin]. In a letter from Sgt. Jon Lacore talking about the enormous amount of waste, he said, "I just can't believe that no one at all is going to jail for this or even being fired or forced to resign."

In my research, I was also shocked to discover the role of contractors in the tragedy of Abu Ghraib [an Iraqi prison where Americans tortured Iraqi inmates]. Its images are seared into the minds of people throughout the world, yet few realize the role of CACI [a company that provides professional and information technology services] and its interrogators. As our team dug deeper and deeper into the numerous contracts, CACI and [its chief executive officer] JP London kept appearing over and over. The Taguba report, the Fay report, and the Human Rights Watch report "By The Numbers" all made clear that CACI had played a significant role in the torture. As Pratap Chatterjee, head of CorpWatch has stated, CACI was using "information technology contracts through the Department of Interior. So either somebody was in a big hurry or they did this deliberately so nobody would ever be able to track this—CACI does a lot of work directly with OSD, Office of the Secretary of Defense."

And even after the investigations, there were no consequences; in fact, CACI continued to receive more and more contracts with no oversight. Later, CACI and JP London were even hired to process cases of fraud and incompetence by contractors! I kid you not—CACI, a corporation that had profited enormously from the war and whose CEO JP London personally made $22,249,453 from his stock and salary in 2004—was being hired to oversee other contractors! This is a madhouse run amuck. And we need your help to fix this.

We know corporations are designed to create significant returns for [their] shareholders. Do we really believe they can and should be fighting for hearts and minds? Do we really think that the corporations with their legal commitment to profitability are to be given the responsibility for some of our country's most critical decisions and actions? Do we want corporations representing us in the battles for our country?

A Peace Movement Honors My Son's Legacy

Cindy Sheehan

In the following selection, war protester Cindy Sheehan delivers a speech opposing the Iraq War and remembering her son Casey, who died in the conflict. Sheehan shares stories with her audience about Casey as a young boy and his decision to join the military. She also expresses her belief that her son would approve of her protest. Sheehan believes that the deaths of soldiers like her son in Iraq can serve a higher purpose: as a starting point to a new peace movement.

I want to tell you a little bit about Casey because this whole movement is because of him and because of the others that have sacrificed themselves. The hardest thing for me to hear, I don't care about them talking about me being a crackpot or a media whore, or a tool of the left, you know. I'm like if I truly was a media whore do you think I would like maybe get myself fixed up a little bit before I went on? That doesn't bother me at all, but what bothers me so much is when they say I am dishonoring my son's memory by what I'm doing, that my son would be ashamed of me or what they really like to say is that I'm pissing, or shitting, or spitting on his grave. And look what Casey, look what Casey has started. You know, I'm here because of Casey, we're all here because of Casey and you know literally there is, there is over 2000 of our brave young people and tens of thousands of innocent Iraqis and I know they are behind us, and I see them, all their faces on your faces.

But Casey was such a gentle kind loving person. He never even got in one fist fight his whole life. Nobody even hated

Cindy Sheehan, "Exclusive: Cindy Sheehan Speaks to Crowd at Camp Casey," *Raw Story*, August 25, 2005. Reproduced by permission of the author.

him enough to punch him let alone kill him, and that's what George Bush did. He put our kids in another person's country and Casey was killed by insurgents. He wasn't killed by terrorists. He was killed by Shiite militia who wanted him out of the country, when Casey was told he was going to be welcomed with chocolate and flowers as a liberator. Well, the people of Iraq saw it differently. They saw him as an occupier.

Remembering Casey

Casey, I want you guys to know about him. You guys know he was an altar boy for 10 years. You guys know he was an eagle scout. You guys know he was an honor student. You guys know he was a very brave person who was scared out of his mind on April 4th, but he went anyway because he said, "Where my chief goes, I go." But you don't know the little boy. He used to come up behind me. He used to wrap his arms around my legs. He'd kiss me on the butt and he'd say, "I wuv you mama." And if he wasn't doing that, he'd walk by and he'd go "dinus ha mama" and that meant, "What are you doing mama?" Every night we'd put him to bed. Every night he would say, "Thank you Mom. This was the best day of my life."

There are a couple of funny stories. Once when he wasn't even 2 it was Easter Sunday and we were all at mass and we were all jammed into one pew, you know there was a bunch of us and the church was full, and we were standing up and we sang the "Lamb of God." We were Catholic and we went to kneel down, and as soon as we knelt down Casey stood up on one of the kneelers and at the top of his voice he goes, "I'm Popeye the sailor man," and everybody in the whole church was cracking up, and so from then on people at our church called him "Popeye." They'd go, "Hey there goes Popeye."

And another cute story was when he was in kindergarten he went to the Catholic school where we went to church and he went to afternoon [session] so we couldn't pull in the parking lot, so we'd have to drive around looking for a place to park. So we were driving around one time and he goes, "Oh mama there's a place," and I said "Oh honey we can't park there it's handicapped," and he goes "Oh, we're not handicapped we're Catholic."

And then, he thought there were only two religions in the world and you guys might know for those of you who grew up Catholic, it's Catholic and public. They thought that those were the two religions. When Casey—in his rebellious years—when we told him something he didn't agree with or whatever, this was the extent of his talking back to us, "thssst." You know seriously this kid was just, just an amazing person and we were so shocked when he joined the Army.

Serving Your Country

I mean, that would have been the last thing we would have expected from Casey, but also the first thing because he always wanted to help. He always wanted to serve. He thought he was giving something back to his country and community, also having been lied to by his recruiter. So, then for my boy to be killed in a war—I don't know if you moms did the same thing, but when I would nurse him I would promise him I would never let him go to war, you know, and I broke that promise to him.

So this is the boy who they say I'm dishonoring by what I do and I know when I get up with Casey, like he went there first before me, when I get up, he's gonna say, "Good job Mom." (applause) He's not going to say, he's not going to say, "Why'd you make me spin in my grave," you know. And I can just hear him saying "George Bush you are really an idiot. You didn't know what you were doing when you killed me. You didn't know what you were getting into." And I'm sure Casey's up there with . . . all the others and they're just going, "Wow, did these guys have moms? They didn't know that this was going to happen when they killed us?"

You know, so Casey, he wanted to get married, everybody thought he would be a priest, but he told me "Mom I want to have a family. I want to get married," and he wanted to be a deacon in the Catholic Church which you can be and be a married person too, and he was told he could be a chaplain's assistant in the army and when he got there they said, you know, "Well, psych is full; you have to be a cook or a humvee mechanic," so he became a humvee mechanic.

He wanted to be an elementary school teacher. He loves kids. He loved animals. He was a very good big brother to Andy, Karly and Janey. And his murder has left a hole in our hearts and in our family, and it's never going to be replaced. No matter how many wonderful people I meet, how many boys that call me "mom," they're not Casey.

Giving Peace a Chance

He used to call me every day from Ft. Hood. I miss that. And . . . like probably for almost a year after he was killed every time the phone rang I'd think, "Oh that's Casey." And so it just like hits you about 50 times a day that you're never going to talk to them, or see them again. And that's why I do what I do, because I can't bear the thought of another mother having to go through the pain that I'm going through. And that's the only reason I do it. So that's what we're here for. We're here because we want to make it so our kids, their deaths stand for peace and love, and this is what is at Camp Casey. And you know some people are saying, "Oh what are guys trying to do, recreate the sixties?" Oh yeah, peace and love is a really bad thing. You know it's been something that's been missing in our country for decades and I'm not ashamed, you know, I'm not ashamed to say that this is a place where you can come and feel loved. You know this is the place where the end of the occupation of Iraq started. This is the place where America comes to say, "We've had enough—enough. You might be able to lie to Congress. You might be able to lie to the media, but you're not lying to us anymore." And this is it, this is where it's going to begin and we're not going [to] stop today, we're not going to stop on the 31st. We're not going [to] stop ever, ever. We will make sure that this keeps on going. We won't have a war, another war, in 30 or 40 years, where we'll be saying, "Oh this is another Iraq." You know, no, it's not going to ever happen again. It's not going to just be me. It's going to be me with the millions of people who are behind us, making sure that that will happen. And you know when this is going to stop? This is going to stop when the mothers say, "No, I'm not giving my son, I'm not giving my son to you so you can kill him to line your pockets," and that's when it's going to stop.

I felt this a lot of times before when Casey was born. I looked in his eyes and it looked like he could tell what I was thinking. That's very disarming when you have like a week old baby looking at you and you know he knows what you're thinking. And I knew he was going to be a great man. I just had no idea how great he was going to be or how much it was going to hurt me. So, thank you Casey and . . . thank you all the others, and I know that they are in heaven and I know that that's why this movement is growing because we have tens of thousands of angels behind us that are supporting us, that are saying, "Well you know we died and that was really crappy, but we hope that our deaths are going to make the world a better place," and it's up to us to make sure that it does. Thank you.

A Soldier's Father Supports the War

Mark Eifert

In the following selection, Mark Eifert describes his and his wife's feelings about having a son who serves in the military in Iraq. Initially, the couple believed that their son would be safer because he had joined the National Guard. Soon, however, they learned that he and other National Guard members were taking a much more active role in the Iraq War. The Eiferts were also disappointed when the National Guard extended their son's deployment by four months. While both parents worry about their son's safety, they believe that the Iraq War is justified and that terrorism must be stopped.

Our youngest son joined the Army National Guard his senior year of high school. As his parents, we had to sign for him to join.

Zach had always shown an interest in the military. When he was younger, he wanted to be a Marine. When he decided to join the National Guard, we were somewhat relieved, thinking that would probably be in a safer branch of the military given the current state of the world. Well, that sure proved to be a misconception on our part.

Zach was deployed in October 2005 to begin training for service in Iraq. That was when our constant fearful feelings started. In the typical military way, we were told very little about what our son's mission would be. Another misconception was that his mission would be a backup/support role. We even heard rumors that our National Guard soldiers would remain in Kuwait, providing only support missions to supply

Mark Eifert, "Iraq from a Parent's Perspective (Part I and Part II)," *Forward Thinking Woman*, May 19, 2007. Copyright © 2007 by Mark Eifert, Fergus Falls, MN. First printed in *Forward Thinking Woman*. Reproduced by permission of the author.

the troops in Iraq. We were disappointed to find out that our soldiers were actually going to a Marine base located in Fallujah in the Al Anbar Province of western Iraq.

Fallujah is known to be a stronghold for al-Qaida and other terrorists and was very dangerous. Our next misconception was that our soldiers would be manning the gates and guard towers on the base, although I do think they actually did that for a short time.

A "Need to Know Basis"

As I said, the military has its own system. We were on a "need to know basis," and we did not need to know. We did learn that the commander of the Marine base in Fallujah was impressed by the capabilities of our National Guard soldiers and so decided to expand their mission, which meant they would take a much more active role in the war on terror.

Their first mission was to stop the mortar attacks the base was experiencing every other day. Our soldiers took the mission to heart, and in short order they had secured the perimeter of the base to the point that terrorist mortars were no longer able to hit within the compound. They swept the area and cleared out weapon and bomb-making caches, as well as capturing known al-Qaida terrorists. Last Thanksgiving they uncovered weapons and bomb-making materials in a cave three miles from the base. The confiscated ordinance covered an area the size of a football field.

Shortly after the first of the year, the soldiers raided a known al-Qaida safe house and torture chamber. They rescued three Iraqis who would have surely been killed. There was also a large weapon and bomb-making cache uncovered at the house.

During this time, several of our soldiers were killed or wounded, some severely. When we received news like that, it was like losing a piece of your heart. Even if you don't know the soldier personally, you know he or she is someone's child, and you relate to that parent's pain and suffering.

Extended Deployment

The ultimate disappointment came early in 2007 when we were expecting our soldiers to come home within the next couple of months. We were counting down the days, when we received the news that our soldiers' deployment would be extended for an additional four months. Rather than coming home in mid-March, now they would not be back until the end of July. The news of the extension was like being punched right in the stomach. I was extremely upset and hurt by the news. We had been on pins and needles for a year hoping and praying that we would not get a phone call saying our son had been wounded or, the worst case scenario, get a personal visit from a military chaplain coming to our door to inform us of our son's death. As I write this on May 19, [2005,] we have another two months of this overwhelming fear. I was devastated. I didn't know how I was going to be able to cope with this additional burden.

Thank the Lord for the great communications we have these days that gives us the ability to talk to our son on a regular basis. Zach called us the day after we found out about the extension and told me not to worry. He said the majority of his buddies did not have a problem being extended—not that they welcomed it, but he said it made sense that they stay longer. They had accomplished so much and had done so much good in that area, making it safer for the soldiers and Iraqi people. They know the area, they know their mission and they can continue the good work they are doing. That made all the difference to me to hear him say those words. It meant so much to him and his buddies to continue making a difference in the world. It still hurt, but after hearing him say what he did and knowing how important it was to him, I could cope after all.

You have your ups and downs being the parent of a soldier in Iraq, but with all the help and support we get from our community and Family Readiness Group, and being able to speak with our son on a regular basis, we get through it.

We are now again counting down the days until they return home.

Misconceptions on the War on Terror

After reading what I just wrote you are probably thinking, "Based on the sacrifice these people are making, they surely do not support '[George W.] Bush's War'!" You would be wrong. This is not Bush's War, this is the global war on terror—and possibly World War III.

We thank God every day that we have a strong leader like President Bush commanding our soldiers and not some weakspine politician who changes position on the war each time a new biased poll is released by a less than truthful media. Poll the soldiers in Iraq and Afghanistan and ask who they would rather have as commander in chief: President Bush or one of the current anti-war leaders in Congress. I would be willing to bet that our current commander in chief would win hands down.

The politicians in Washington as well as the many so-called troop supporters attending peace rallies are doing more harm than they can imagine. Their anti-war speech affects the morale of our troops, and the soldiers see first-hand how the terrorist[s] are embolden[ed] by it.

From the beginning, the terrorist battle plan to defeat America was based on the belief that Americans do not have the stomach for a long war, and with the news media only focusing on stories that oppose the war, the terrorists are watching CNN and thinking their plan is working. Wake up, America! We cannot lose this war, and we need to change your plan for withdrawal and defeat to a plan of victory. We need to give our soldiers everything they need to win. If we do not, these terrorist animals will be beheading us on the streets of our American cities.

Stopping Extremists

My theory is that most Americans have not sacrificed enough at this point to believe the importance of winning this war. By the time they do, I pray it is not too late to save our way of life and freedom.

Most Americans are aware of the war and they think, "It's terrible, but it's way over there. It hasn't had any real, personal effect on my lifestyle, so it will take care of itself. I don't need to be concerned."

Wake up, America! It is going to affect your lifestyle if we do not stop these radical al-Qaida extremists.

If I could have one wish, other than having my son come home safe and sound, I would wish we could stop all the vicious anti-war, hate speech we now have in this country. It degrades our people, our leaders and our country. America is the greatest nation this world has ever seen. We all need to be proud to be Americans and unite when we are threatened and our freedom jeopardized.

Yes, as Americans we have different opinions about this war—differing opinions are part of what makes us great—and our soldiers are fighting and dying to preserve our right to be different. But please, let's make it clear to the world that while we may have differing opinions among ourselves, we are the United States of America, with the emphasis on *United*.

Organizations to Contact

The editors have compiled the following list of organizations concerned with the issues debated in this book. The descriptions are derived from materials provided by the organizations. All have publications or information available for interested readers. The list was compiled on the date of publication of the present volume; the information provided here may change. Be aware that many organizations take several weeks or longer to respond to inquiries, so allow as much time as possible.

American Enterprise Institute (AEI)
1150 Seventeenth St. NW, Washington, DC   20036
(202) 862-5800
Web site: www.aei.org

The American Enterprise Institute for Public Policy Research is a scholarly research institute that is dedicated to preserving limited government, private enterprise, and a strong foreign policy and national defense. Its publications on Iraq include articles in its magazine *American Enterprise* and books including *Study of Revenge: The First World Trade Center Attack and Saddam Hussein's War Against America*. Articles, speeches, and seminar transcripts on Iraq are available on the AEI Web site.

Association of the United States Army (AUSA)
2425 Wilson Blvd., Arlington, VA   22201
toll-free: (800) 336-4570
e-mail: info@ausa.org
Web site: www.ausa.org

The AUSA is a private nonprofit educational organization with multiple chapters around the world. The organization supports members of the United States Army, National Guard, Reserve, civilians, retirees, and family members, and maintains an active legislative agenda. The AUSA also publishes *Army Magazine*.

The Brookings Institution
1775 Massachusetts Ave. NW, Washington, DC   20036
(202) 797-6000 • fax: (202) 797-6004
e-mail: brookinfo@brookings.edu
Web site: www.brookings.org

The institution, founded in 1927, is a think-tank that conducts research and education in foreign policy, economics, government, and the social sciences. In 2001 it began America's Response to Terrorism, a project that provides briefings and analysis to the public and which is featured on the center's Web site. Its publications include the quarterly *Brookings Review*, periodic *Policy Briefs*, and books such as *Terrorism and U.S. Foreign Policy*.

Center for Strategic and International Studies (CSIS)
1800 K St. NW, Washington, DC   20006
(202) 887-0200 • fax: (202) 775-3199
Web site: www.csis.org

Founded in 1962, the center is a bipartisan nonprofit organization that works to provide world leaders with strategic insights and policy options on current and emerging global issues. It publishes books such as *The "Instant" Lessons of the Iraq War*; a journal on political, economic, and security issues, the *Washington Quarterly*; and other publications, including reports that can be downloaded from its Web site.

Education for Peace in Iraq Center (EPIC)
1101 Pennsylvania Ave. SE, Washington, DC   20003
(202) 543-6176
e-mail: info@epic-usa.org
Web site: http://epic-usa.org/

EPIC works to improve humanitarian conditions in Iraq and protect the human rights of Iraq's people. It opposed both international economic sanctions and U.S. military action against Iraq. Articles on Iraq are available on its Web site, including *The Ground Truth Project*, a series featuring interviews with soldiers, Iraqis, and aid workers.

Hoover Institution

434 Galvez Mall, Stanford University
Stanford, CA 94305-6010
(650) 723-1754 • fax: (650) 723-1687
Web site: www.hoover.org

Founded in 1919 by later U.S. president Herbert Hoover, the Hoover Institution is a public policy research center devoted to the advanced study of politics, economics, and political economy—both domestic and foreign—as well as international affairs. It publishes the quarterly *Hoover Digest*, which often includes articles on Iraq, the Middle East, and the war on terrorism, as well as a newsletter and special reports.

The Iraq Foundation

1012 Fourteenth St. NW, Ste. 1110, Washington, DC 20012
(202) 347-4662 • fax: (202) 347-7897
e-mail: iraq@iraqfoundation.org
Web site: www.iraqfoundation.org

The Iraq Foundation is a nonprofit nongovernmental organization that works for democracy and human rights in Iraq and for a better international understanding of Iraq's potential as a contributor to political stability and economic progress in the Middle East. The Iraq Foundation publishes a monthly newsletter and conducts a number of projects, including the Human Rights Advocacy Initiative and Widows Empowerment Project.

Iraq War Veterans Organization, Inc.

PO Box 571, Yucaipa, CA 92399
e-mail: stories@iraqwarveterans.org
Web site: www.iraqwarveterans.org

The Iraq War Veterans Organization actively supports the welfare of the community and to assist disabled veterans of the U.S. Armed Forces. The organization actively collects war stories from both veterans and active duty soldiers, and its Web site includes information pertaining to filing disability claims.

Middle East Forum

1500 Walnut St., Ste. 1050, Philadelphia, PA   19102
(215) 546-5406 • fax: (215) 546-5409
e-mail: info@meforum.org
Web site: www.meforum.org

The Middle East Forum is a think-tank that works to define and promote American interests in Iraq and other parts of the Middle East. It supports strong American ties with Israel, Turkey, and other democracies as they emerge. It publishes the *Middle East Quarterly*, a policy-oriented journal, and *Campus Watch*, which monitors biased teaching by U.S. professors about the Middle East. Its Web site includes articles on Iraq and other topics as well as a discussion forum.

Middle East Media Research Institute (MEMRI)

PO Box 27837, Washington, DC   20038-7837
(202) 955-9070 • fax: (202) 955-9077
e-mail: memri@memri.org
Web site: www.memri.org

Founded in 1998, MEMRI translates and disseminates articles and commentaries from Middle East media sources and provides analysis on the political, ideological, intellectual, social, cultural, and religious trends in the region. MEMRI also offers analysis of political and cultural trends in the Middle East on its Web site.

Middle East Policy Council

1730 M St. NW, Ste. 512, Washington, DC   20036-4505
(202) 296-6767 • fax: (202) 296-5791
e-mail: info@mepc.org
Web site: www.mepc.org

The Middle East Policy Council was founded in 1981 to expand public discussion and understanding of issues affecting U.S. policy in the Middle East. The council is a nonprofit educational organization that operates nationwide. Articles on Iraq can be found in the *Middle East Policy Journal*, its quarterly publication, and in the Capital Hill Conference Series, also a quarterly publication. The council also supports the Public Outreach and Education Program, a nationwide effort to promote a better understanding of the Middle East in secondary and postsecondary schools.

Middle East Research and Information Project (MERIP)

1500 Massachusetts Ave. NW, Ste. 119
Washington, DC   20005
(202) 223-3677 • fax: (202) 223-3604
Web site: www.merip.org

MERIP is a nonprofit nongovernmental organization with no links to any religious, educational, or political organizations in the United States or elsewhere. Its mission is to educate the public about the contemporary Middle East with particular emphasis on U.S. foreign policy, human rights, and social justice issues. It publishes the bimonthly *Middle East Report*. Other publications include *Why Another War? A Backgrounder on the Iraq Crisis.*

United States Department of State, Bureau of Near Eastern Affairs

2201 C St. NW, Washington, DC   20520
(202) 647-4000
Web site: www.state.gov/p/nea/

The bureau deals with U.S. foreign policy and U.S. relations with the countries in the Middle East, including Iraq. Its Web site offers country information as well as news briefings and press statements on U.S. foreign policy, and includes a Youth and Education section. The bureau has also generated a series of *Background Notes*, offering economic, political, and historical information on a variety of countries.

Washington Institute for Near East Policy

1828 L St. NW, Ste. 1050, Washington, DC   20036
(202) 452-0650 • fax: (202) 223-5364

e-mail: info@washingtoninstitute.org
Web site: www.washingtoninstitute.org

The institute is an independent nonprofit research organization that provides information and analysis on the Middle East and U.S. policy in that region. It publishes numerous books, including *How to Build a New Iraq After Saddam*, as well as policy papers and reports on regional politics, security, and economics. Its Web site includes a special Focus on Iraq section that features articles and reports on that nation.

For Further Research

Books

Ali A. Allawi, *The Occupation of Iraq: Winning the War, Losing the Peace*. New Haven, CT: Yale University Press, 2007.

Matthew Currier Burden, *The Blog of War: Front-Line Dispatches from Soldiers in Iraq and Afghanistan*. New York: Simon & Schuster, 2006.

Colby Buzzell, *My War: Killing Time in Iraq*. New York: Berkley, 2005.

Richard Engel, *War Journal: My Five Years in Iraq*. New York: Simon & Schuster, 2008.

Rick Fawn and Raymond A. Hinnebusch, *The Iraq War: Causes and Consequences*. Boulder, CO: Lynne Rienner, 2006.

Dexter Filkens, *The Forever War*. New York: Knopf, 2008.

David Finkle, *The Good Soldiers*. New York: Farrar, Straus, and Giroux, 2009.

Seth W.B. Folsom, *The Highway War: A Marine Company Commander in Iraq*. Dulles, VA: Potomac Books, 2006.

Peter W. Galbraith, *The End of Iraq: How American Incompetence Created a War Without End*. New York: Simon & Schuster, 2007.

Richard N. Haass, *War of Necessity, War of Choice: A Memoir of Two Iraq Wars*. New York: Simon & Schuster, 2009.

Michael Isikoff and David Corn, *Hubris: The Inside Story of Spin, Scandal, and the Selling of the Iraq War*. New York: Three Rivers, 2007.

Tim Pritchard, *Ambush Alley: The Most Extraordinary Battle of the Iraq War*. New York: Presidio, 2007.

Thomas E. Ricks, *Fiasco: The American Military Adventure in Iraq*. New York: Penguin, 2006.

Ryan Smithson, *Ghosts of War: The True Story of a 19-Year-Old GI*. New York: HarperCollins, 2009.

Bing West, *No True Glory: A Frontline Account of the Battle of Fallujah*. New York: Bantam, 2006.

Bing West, *The Strongest Tribe: War, Politics, and the End-game in Iraq*. New York: Random House, 2008.

Michael Yon, *Moment of Truth in Iraq: How a New "Greatest Generation" of American Soldiers Is Turning Defeat and Disaster into Victory and Hope*. Minneapolis: Richard Vigilante Books, 2008.

Periodicals

Tim Adams, "The Nation's Conscience," *New Statesman*, June 8, 2009.

P. Ryan Baber, "The War on TV," *Hollywood Reporter*, June 2, 2009.

Jonathan P. Baird, "Learn the Lessons of Vietnam," *New Hampshire Business Review*, September 25, 2009.

Nellie Gonzalez Cutler, "A Way Out of Iraq," *Time for Kids*, April 3, 2009.

James Delingpole, "Utterly Gripped," *Spectator*, June 20, 2009.

David Denby, "Death Calls," *New Yorker*, November 16, 2009.

David Denby, "Life Battles," *New Yorker*, June 29, 2009.

Pamela Lewis Dolan, "Video Games Used to Treat Posttraumatic Stress," *American Medical News*, September 28, 2009.

Anthony Fenton, "Canada's Outsourced War: Think We Never Went to Iraq? Think Again," *This Magazine*, September–October 2009.

Bill Hallman, "In the Line of Fire: Running the Baghdad Office Presents Some . . . Special Managerial Challenges," *American Lawyer*, August 2009.

Joe Klein, "The Mystery of the Surge," *Time*, November 23, 2009.

Jon Meacham, "Know Thy Enemy. And Then Defeat Him," *Newsweek*, October 5, 2009.

Greg Mitchell, "Six Years Ago Today: Media Hailed 'End of Iraq War,'" *Editor & Publisher*, April 9, 2009.

Mackubin Thomas Owen, "The Learning Curve; Rediscovering Counterinsurgency in Iraq," *Weekly Standard*, May 11, 2009.

Carol Pipes, "Finding God in Iraq: How He's Mending and Moving in This War-Torn Nation," *Today's Christian Woman*, July–August 2009.

Scott Taylor, "Damaging Democracy . . . British Style," *Esprit de Corps*, April 2009.

Paul Wells, "And Now . . . a Loopy Iraq War Movie," *Maclean's*, July 27, 2009.

Peter Wilby, "No Room for Closure," *New Statesman*, June 22, 2009.

Fareed Zakaria, "Victory in Iraq," *Newsweek*, June 15, 2009.

Index